THE STUFFED STOAT

JOSEPHINE FERGUSON

with illustrations by Moira Hoddell.

Published by

MELROSE BOOKS

An Imprint of Melrose Press Limited
St Thomas Place, Ely
Cambridgeshire
CB7 4GG, UK
www.melrosebooks.com

FIRST EDITION

Cover designed by Matt Stephens

Illustrations by Moira Hoddell
Illustrations on pages 14 and 18 by Josephine Ferguson.

ISBN 978-1-906561-70-3

Printed and bound in Great Britain by:
CPI Antony Rowe, Chippenham, Wiltshire

FSC
Mixed Sources
Product group from well-managed
forests and other controlled sources
Cert no. SGS-COC-2953
www.fsc.org
© 1996 Forest Stewardship Council

CONTENTS

PART 1: THE END OF AN ERA

1916	1
Wedding in Gwalior	3
Hove, near Brighton, England, 1934	5
Hove, Mud Pies and Murder	12
The South Africans and Lord Hullin's Daughter	19
Kaffirs or Camels?	22
Pauleen, the Orang-Outang and the Crisis	25
Goodbye to Granny – and to Peace	29

PART 2: THE STUFFED STOAT: AN EXCELLENT EDUCATION

Prologue: 1938	33
1940 – "Take Me to Ditchling …"	35
The Bell, the Club and the Iron Bar	38
The 'Ogress'	41
Lunching on Bébé Mort	44
Hitler Ends an Era	48
Scrambled Blackberry Pie	50
British Jellyhood	54
I Join the Axis Powers	56
"Goodbye Ditchling – Hallo Hassocks"	59
The Scarlet Pimpernel	64
The Cheeky Loaf	66
Miss Mary: Literature and Morals	67
Letters from India	71
The Red Ribbon	73
An Epitaph of Laughter	76

THE STUFFED STOAT

In the Fever Hospital	78
The Warrior Returns	80
Back to School in Ditchling	84
Geoffrey and Hiawatha	88
Fishing Lessons	91
My Teaching Career	96
Definition of a Lady	98
Epilogue	101
Miss Mary's Parting Present Epilogue by Robert Browning	103

PART 3: AFTER THE WAR

What are You Doing Now?	107
Death	111
The Lord's in the Garden	114
From Mucking Out to Planting Out	117
Typing to the Teddy Bears' Picnic	120
Fleet Street	125
Water, Water Everywhere and Far Too Much to Drink	142

PART 1:

THE END OF AN ERA

1916

Along the drive of Hyderabad Residency the solemn funeral procession slowly crawled, the pall-bearers carrying the late Resident, Sir Alexander Pinhey, Knight Commander of The Star of India, to his final resting place in the Residency grounds, where his faithful Indian servant had built a tomb for him. The untimely death, from enteric fever, of this popular and promising man, said to have been tipped to be the next Viceroy, was indeed a great shock and tragedy to all around him, Indian and British alike. He was just 54 years old, and had devoted his life to the welfare of the Indian people.

In the silence of the sultry air, a distant buzzing sound could be heard approaching ... Suddenly, all was chaos and confusion, as swarms of bees descended from the trees flanking the drive and attacked the pall-bearers and those around them. The kindly Resident had always protected the bees, whose nests were in the tall trees, and had ordered them to be left alone whenever anyone had suggested exterminating them, and now it seemed that the bees, with their uncanny intuition, had realised that their protector was being taken away for ever, and were making a last, desperate effort to get him back.

This, then, was the chaotic send-off to my grandfather's short but brilliant life, and perhaps he would forgive me for suggesting that a suitable epitaph might have been, 'Death, where is thy sting?'

Now, only the huge photograph albums remain, containing enormous sepia groups of famous people – King George V and Queen Mary, Lord Shaftesbury, Lord Crichton, Colvin, Dugdale, etc., etc., together with the Visitors' Book with the Royal signatures in it. A quaint old picture of my grandparents entertaining the Royal couple when they were Prince and Princess of Wales in 1905 now hangs in the entrance hall of our humble cottage, amongst the muddy gardening tools. One of our more recent guests remarked that she did so enjoy coming to see us, as we were the only people she knew who had Queen Mary's signature in the lavatory ... (Owing to lack of space, we had had to put a bookcase in the 'downstairs cloaks'.)

The tragedy of her husband's sudden death left Lady Pinhey a widow when still in her forties, and brought her wonderful life in India to an abrupt end. From the brilliant Residency in Hyderabad she retreated to a flat in South Kensington.

However, before leaving India there was one happy event to cheer her, and that was the wedding of her second daughter to one of the Officers stationed at the Residency. In the sad circumstances it was perforce a quiet wedding, although this was the first of her children to get married.

The Pioneer newspaper of Saturday, October 7th, 1916, contained the following report:

WEDDING IN GWALIOR

O N THURSDAY THE 5TH OF OCTOBER AT St. Peter's Church, Moran, Gwalior, a very pretty wedding was solemnised between Miss Violet Pinhey (the younger daughter of the late Colonel Sir Alexander Fleetwood Pinhey, K.C.S.I., C.I.E., and Lady Pinhey) and Captain Herbert Stewart Phillips of the 27th Light Cavalry (son of the late Colonel H. W. Phillips and Mrs Phillips, Stokefield, Great Malvern).

Great interest was taken in the wedding, Sir Alexander being so well-known in Gwalior, having been Resident there. Owing to his recent death, the wedding was naturally a very quiet one.

The bride, who was given away by Colonel G. H. D. Gimlette, I.M.S., looked very pretty in a simple frock of soft white satin, draped with Honiton lace, lent for the occasion by her mother. She wore a ninon and Honiton lace cap, caught up at the four corners with little bunches of orange blossom, and a ninon veil. The bridegroom, like his best man, was in khaki.

The service was conducted by the Ven. Archdeacon Price, who had come from Nagpur for the purpose, assisted by the Reverend W. Lugard Clarke from Sanigor. It is many years since the old Morar Cantonment Church, which had been prettily decorated for the occasion by Mrs H. M. Ball, had seen a military wedding.

The company included His Highness the Maharaja Scindia and Suite, and Lady Pinhey, the mother of the bride, Miss Pinhey, sister of the bride, Mr W. G. Jardine, the Resident, Sir Michael and Lady Filose and Miss Beatrice Filose, Mr and Mrs Malan, cousins of the bride, Mr and Mrs Waterfield, Colonel and Mrs Birdwood, Captain Elliot Colvin and many other old friends.

At the conclusion of the ceremony, the bride and bridegroom and the wedding guests drove off to the Palace where a reception was held by his Highness the Maharaja. His Highness proposed the health of the happy pair, Captain Phillips returning thanks. The bride then cut the cake with her husband's sword, and shortly afterwards they departed by motor, under showers of rice and 'other parting presents' en route for Tigra, a shooting box kindly lent by His Highness the Maharaja, where the first part of the honeymoon is to be spent.'

Barely a year after returning to England, tragedy struck again for Lady

Pinhey when the eldest of her three sons was killed in the trenches in 1917. Somehow she pulled herself together and, at the instance of Lord and Lady Willingdon (Lord Willingdon was then Governor of Bombay), she was asked to take charge of the children of the Maharaja of Patiala while they were being educated in England, and went to live with them at (East) Sheen. Even now, getting on for 100 years later, I, her grand-daughter, still come across the odd blanket bearing a name-tape with 'Patiala' on it.

'London Granny', as we knew her, was the tenth and youngest child of General Sir Henry Gordon, elder brother of General Charles Gordon, hero of China and Khartoum. In India she had gained quite a reputation for her sparkling wit, originality and ability to remember the important details about people. The greatest part of her interests was always in India, and from India she delighted to welcome old friends. I still retain a clear, child's-eye view of her London flat, filled with those Indian friends, drinking cups of tea and talking volubly. Such names as Chattagee, Muckagee and Ah Sing lodged themselves in my memory from the age of four.

What would the future hold for her children and their descendants? Only one, her eldest grandson, would eventually become an Ambassador and receive the red-carpet treatment, albeit in various turbulent Middle Eastern embassies, which were not so glittering as India …

(His much younger sister, however, owing to a combination of circumstances and a complete lack of 'push', was to descend to the shallows of extreme serfdom on a typewriter …)

Hove, near Brighton, England, 1934

T HE ORGAN-GRINDER'S MONKEY EXTENDED A DARK BROWN paw as if to scratch the child, who recoiled, screaming in terror with the full force of her four-year-old lungs, not daring to stroke it again for many months. However, with time, fear of the monkey would recede, but the pleasantly monotonous tinkling of the barrel organ, echoing down the street of tall Victorian houses, would always return to evoke childhood memories …

Some of these memories were frightening, like the time when she put a blue bead up her nose and pushed it as far as she could: four adults had held her down on the floor and put pepper up her nose until she sneezed and, miraculously, the bead had dropped out. The pepper had been the brilliant idea of her youngest uncle, Elliot, the fifth and last child of London Granny, called Elliot because it was the family name of his Godmother, Lady Minto.

Another time she had climbed a ladder, left against the high garden wall, to see what Tommy, the stammering boy next door, was doing … The next minute, her father and mother were picking her up off the ground and murmuring a new word – *concussion*.

Most of the memories were happy ones, of long sunny days on the beach. It is strange how wet days are completely erased from the memory: childhood was permanent summer.

The barrel organ was the daily accompaniment to the family's walk down Tisbury Road, past the Town Hall whose clock played *Rule Britannia* and *Men of Harlech* at various times of day, across Church Road and on, down to the sea. All in all, it was a musical road, as Mr Barrence, the milkman, treated his customers to operatic arias, sung in a rich baritone above the clinking of the milk bottles.

Mrs Phillips' habit of walking at top speed was a family joke, and neighbours must have commented on the early morning sighting of a worried little woman, rushing down the road towards the sea, hotly pursued by a collection of small children, running to keep up with her. There were not just the three of us, but very often other people's children who were left in her care when their parents were in India, or foreign boys who paid to stay with us while they studied English. That was how our mother supplemented our father's meagre Army pension after he was invalided out of his Indian Cavalry Regiment (the 27th Light Cavalry) in 1929, having sustained 14 fractures and lost an eye in a private plane crash of which he was the sole survivor. It just seemed quite normal to me that he wore a black patch like a pirate. Little boys used to run up to him in the street and say, "'Ullo Nelson" and run away again. However, when my mother first met him as a tall, young subaltern in Hyderabad, his pale blue and silver uniform setting off his black hair and blue eyes, he must have looked quite dashing.

Every fine morning we would be roused with the announcement that we were going to have a bathe in the sea before breakfast, afterwards eating bacon sandwiches on the beach, teeth chattering as a result of the sudden immersion in cold salt water. My mother suffered from acute modesty, and I think her preference for early morning swimming arose from the fact that there were very few people around at that time to see her clad only in a bathing suit.

Later in the day we would meet our little friends in the public gardens near the seafront, officially named King's Gardens, but known to us simply as 'the gardens', where we played on smooth lawns or rode 'fairy-cycles' – the first-size bikes to which we aspired after tricycles. Having a fairy-cycle was a status symbol akin to owning a Rolls Royce, and I did not have one … I still had an ancient tricycle.

I suppose they weren't really public gardens, any more than public schools are public, because our parents had to have a key to the gate, for which, presumably, they must have paid an annual fee, although we children never knew about such things. It wasn't 'nice' to talk about money – and our family never had any: in those days it didn't matter if you were penniless as long as you *pronounced* everything properly.

While we played our innocent games in the sunshine of the early thirties, little did we know that those were the last serene and carefree days before England would change for ever because a power-crazed Austrian painter with a ridiculous moustache decided that he wanted to conquer the world.

Our mothers, who all addressed each other as 'Mrs' – Smith, Jones, etc. (in our case more likely Carruthers, Paget-Tomlinson or Carew-Smythe) – but *never* by Christian names until they had known each other for at least three years, sat in the elegant wood-and-glass shelters with seats on either side, protected from the wind, and talked of India …

In particular, my mother recalled the Delhi Durbar of 1911, which she had attended with her parents when she was 17. My grandmother's scrapbook, meticulously kept, contains every souvenir imaginable of the Delhi Durbar: all the special timetables, invitations to other camps, official instructions as to procedure, badges for certain enclosures and huge sepia photographs from *The Sphere* magazine, together with newspaper cuttings. A feast of nostalgia …

There can be few people alive now, if any, who attended that magnificent event, probably the most colourful and glorious in all India's history, but my mother spoke of it constantly. Her father, being Resident of the largest State in India – Hyderabad Deccan – had to be the first of the Residents to go up and make his bow to the new King-Emperor, George V, in company with the young Nizam (pronounced Nizz-arm) who had recently succeeded his late father, mainly thanks to my grandfather, who had discovered and averted a plot to prevent his succession.

On the 11th of November, 1911, King George and Queen Mary set sail for India to attend the Durbar a month later. People in England today have a misinformed impression of the 'arrogant, imperialistic British Raj', sitting back, 'chota peg' in hand, being waited on by Indian servants, but my grandfather and his colleagues in the Indian Political Service were genuine, dedicated, hard working people, trying to help the people of India to be educated in local government until they could govern themselves. They had a deep love of India, and the effort and organisation which they put into the preparations for the amazing Durbar were probably even greater than those here in London before our present Queen's coronation.

Dur*bar* (the accent is on the second syllable and the word originates from the Hindi *darbar*) means a court – of a native ruler or governor in India – or a levée at that court. The Indians meant to show the new King-Emperor all the splendours of their country in the most magnificent style possible.

Delhi had a normal population of 233,000. The total number of people pouring into the city for this event was estimated at well over a million, only 21,000 of which were Europeans, including 16,500 British soldiers. It was very rarely that even large towns and cities could provide house-room for any abnormal influx of people, so the first necessity was to form a great encampment for those who came from outside. In the West, the idea of camping is generally associated with the hard necessities of war or travel, but the East, especially India, has always been a world of tents and nomad life.

Camps were set up for the representatives from each State; the Princes, the Governors, the Army, principal merchants, members of local bodies, etc. The difficulties were very great: land had to be acquired; some of it, liable to flooding from the river Jumna, had to be drained, trees cut down, growers of standing crops had to be compensated, cavalry cantonments moved elsewhere, new roads built, camp sites marked and gardens planted.

The area involved was 45 square miles, including 30 villages. The King-Emperor's own camp was the nucleus, with the most important people having their camps nearest to his, the other camps spreading outwards in decreasing seniority. Wide roads divided the camps from each other and a special railway ran through the camp with a station for each separate group.

Forty-four miles of line were constructed, 29 miles of sidings, 64 level-crossings, 14 bridges and 29 fully-equipped stations, to quote just *some* of the statistics mentioned in the signed copy of the Official Historical Record of the Imperial Visit, which was left to me.

Within the space of four days, no fewer than 190 special trains from all parts of India converged on the camp in addition to a normal daily traffic of 256 trains. Each camp had its own provision of motors and carriages and there was a central garage with petrol and repair shops for all.

All these matters and many more, such as telephones, telegraphs and posts, were organised by those British officials who achieved, in unaccustomed heat, a fantastic system which ran like clockwork. The telephone line had 2,352 miles (exclusive of 500 miles connected with the railways) handling over 1,000 calls an hour during the active part of the day.

When the great day arrived, the procession consisted of 186 carriages and 10,000 men. The troops were arranged round the King-Emperor in geometric designs, making a gorgeous colour scheme. The procession was over five miles long and took three hours to pass along the route. The sight was an experience which my mother never forgot; it must have been the greatest spectacle of her life. The main object was for all the Chiefs and dignitaries (having parked their carriages in pre-arranged places) to pay homage to Their Majesties by going up individually to bow before them.

There were 161 Chiefs, and the first to come was the young Nizam of Hyderabad with my grandfather in a four-horse landau with *syces* (grooms) in yellow liveries (the colour of the House of Hyderabad). The rulers of Hyderabad have always been most loyal to the British.

I cannot describe the whole of that glorious day, but at the end of it, *The Sphere* of 6th January, 1912, described how 'The Indian night was lit with unsurpassed illuminations'.

The administration had been so impeccable that there had not been a single hitch or accident.

After the Durbar the King and Queen travelled extensively through India, being welcomed cordially wherever they went, and were away from England for three months altogether. My grandmother said that when they stayed with her, they liked nothing better than to go up to their room and read their children's letters from England, because they missed them so much.

It is sad that the present generation has been encouraged to regard the British Raj as something to jeer at and be ashamed of. The notion of an Empire in which both Europeans and Asiatics should be ruled by a monarch who was indifferent to the distinction between them and was looked on by all equally as their sovereign, was actually formed over 2,000 years ago by Alexander the Great, but it did not come into being until Queen Victoria's intuitive sympathies and instinctive statesmanship achieved it.

For the first time in history India enjoyed a quarter of a century of complete peace within its borders; education and medical relief were brought within reach of all, communications were increased 1,000 times, the spectre of famine was hunted down, unsurpassed schemes for material advancement were carried out and prosperity was such as had never been known.

The aim of the British was to organise India for peaceful development within, and to fortify it for efficient resistance to pressure from without; Lord Curzon, when Viceroy, said that his chief desire was to show that participation in the Empire involved responsibilities as well as rights, and that the links which held it together were *not* "iron fetters forged for the weak by the strong ..."

When our mothers were not reminiscing about India, they were either having coffee in Forfar's in Church Road, or tea in each other's houses while we listened like hawks to the grown-ups' conversation. Children of the present day no longer do this, and I think it is a pity, because they only mix with their peers, therefore learning nothing much, whereas we picked up a lot of general knowledge and a few more 'grown-up' words from listening to our elders (even if we did not know what they meant).

I went in fear of a rather unpleasant child who wanted to be a boy, and wore grey flannel shorts. She invariably arrived in King's Gardens with her gang of toughs, who took up a menacing position, standing above the rest of us on one of the garden seats, waving sticks about in a threatening manner.

My mother and father (now a Major) had not gone immediately to Hove from India. Life, for me, their 'afterthought', had started in a Sussex village called Storrington, about a year after they had returned from India with my two elder brothers, John and David. Of that early life I remember nothing, but I gather that my arrival went something like this: "Another lovely boy, Mrs P," announced the doctor enthusiastically – and inaccurately.

According to my mother, those were the first words which I might have heard above my own yells as I entered this world. A mistake from the beginning, which seems to have set the pattern for a lifetime of errors and wrong decisions, although they all seemed a good idea at the time. Perhaps Fate really does have it all mapped out for us in advance? Some day it may add up, and every incident will have contributed to Life's (in my case) rather badly-stitched and far from rich tapestry.

The doctor's slight error was really the second mistake: my parents had not intended to have any more children. My brothers were already 12 and almost eight years old; they had both been born in India. John, the elder of the two, was away at prep-school and, in a letter, had thoughtfully provided our mother with the address of a midwife which he had noticed on a brass plate when out for a walk with the school crocodile.

David was at home, but complained that he had missed my arrival because he was in the lavatory. My father was downstairs, busily consuming the brandy which had been bought to relieve my mother's agony.

The doctor's original inaccurate announcement had been prompted by his first glimpse of my broad shoulders, which have for ever been the bane of my life, causing me to look square-shaped instead of willowy and elegant, as I should have liked, although, metaphorically speaking, I have *needed* broad shoulders …

Cobb Cottage, in which I was born, was a pretty, whitewashed little house, standing back in its garden at the edge of a track leading through pine woods, just off the Amberley Road at Storrington. Originally called 'Storing Town', it was said to have been used by smugglers who came through a tunnel under the South Downs and stored their contraband there. Just a small village in those days, it has now expanded into a much larger and less attractive place. My mother had spent some of her childhood staying with an aunt who owned the Manor House (since demolished) in the days when Parham Park was 'Lord Zouch's Park' and Storrington College boasted Anthony Eden, Jomo Kenyatta and the Duke of Norfolk as its pupils, as well as my mother's eldest brother and cousins.

By a strange coincidence, my father's ancestor, Sir Herbert Stewart (after whom he was named) was killed trying to rescue my mother's ancestor, General Gordon. My father's mother, Mary Stewart, was the great-granddaughter of the 7th Earl of Galloway, Clan Chief of the Stewarts. The 4th Earl was a cousin of Lord Darnley, who married Mary Queen of Scots. I now have the painting of that ill-fated queen, which used to hang in my grandmother's dining-room in Cheltenham.

'Cheltenham Granny' married a Colonel Phillips who was in the 50th Regiment, The Queen's Own. He became Chief Paymaster, British Forces, Egypt, but died of pneumonia at Exeter when on leave, aged 60, leaving seven children, four girls and three boys, of whom my father was the eldest son.

My mother's father, 'Alick' Pinhey (pronounced Pinny), came from a long line of Devon farmers who farmed the land at Blackawton, near Dartmouth, for about 300 years. The church register mentions the marriage of a 'Pynhey' in 1542. Alick's father, Robert, married the daughter of the Vicar, the Reverend the Honourable Edward Pellew, son of Admiral Viscount Exmouth. This Robert Pinhey was not a farmer, but became a judge of the High Court in

Bombay, so I suppose that is why my grandfather went to India and joined the Indian Political Service.

The Exmouths (Pellews) were cousins of the Sidmouths (family name Addington) and my mother kept in touch with all these cousins when her boys were small, sometimes taking them to stay at the respective family seats in Devon – Canonteign and Upottery – but I never met any of them because World War II started and prevented much travelling about.

So, with all these illustrious and historically interesting ancestors, here I was, being born in a rented cottage in Sussex, all set to lead a quiet, rural life, and really, who could ask for anything better?

After leaving the Indian Army as a Major, my father was never fit enough to work again, and in those days it 'wasn't done' for a retired officer and gentleman to take a job, so he began to take an interest in the garden, entering his produce in the local flower show and becoming more keen as success came in the shape of regular first prizes for onions and sweet peas. I inherited this passion: as soon as I was on my feet, I began to 'help' him … This included staggering the length of the border, pulling out all the tulip bulbs which he had planted so laboriously …

Luckily, I could not understand what he said. This was my first attempt at gardening. Despite this fiasco, he continued to encourage me to take an interest in horticulture. At his suggestion my dolls were called Dandelion, Cauliflower and Antirrhinum. Dandelion was an ugly, hairless rag doll, wearing a red and black check frock, Cauliflower was rather pretty, slim, with long legs (as I would have liked to be) and Antirrhinum was small but well-dressed.

My father's passion for gardening has been a far greater legacy to me than money would have been: it has been a comforting, all-absorbing therapy throughout my later life, as well as a source of income in time of trouble. I have had many other jobs, but always returned at intervals with great joy and enthusiasm to the soil; whenever life became too depressing I took to the Great Outdoors. To be fair, this could also have been attributable to the genes of the Devon farmers …

Hove, Mud Pies and Murder

WHEN I WAS TWO YEARS OLD WE moved, rather reluctantly, to Hove, the better, residential end of Brighton. We hated leaving the country, but beggars couldn't be choosers, and my great-aunt was *giving* us a house!

The eldest of the 10 Gordon children, she was known as 'Aunt Queenie' because she looked like Queen Victoria. She had been left the house by a friend, and as she already owned and inhabited another house in Hove, she very kindly gave the inherited one to my mother, who was her Goddaughter. It contained huge and hideous furniture, plus an Aspidistra in the hall. How we would have managed without that house I don't know, as my father's Army pension barely covered the rent of a cottage, and he was not very good at holding on to money, anyway. (There is one village in Sussex where my brother has always said "Duck when you pass the grocer" because my father left there owing £40 – a large sum in the late twenties.) Earlier still, he had kept eight hunters and a pack of hounds while a Captain on half-pay during one of his periods of sick leave …

John won a Classics scholarship to Brighton College at this time, which was another good reason for our move to Hove. My father had wanted him to go to *his* old school, Sherborne, but in those days you had to accept or decline immediately the first scholarship you were offered, and the decision had to be made before John even sat the exam for Sherborne.

A bird in the hand is worth two in the bush, thought our parents, so off he went to Brighton, where he did very well, eventually becoming Head Boy and Captain of Rugger, finally leaving with an Exhibition to Oxford.

David remained a boarder at the family prep-school in Horsham – Springfield Park – which had been started by our great-uncle by marriage, Gerald Blunt (related to Wilfred Blunt) who had married one of our Gordon grandmother's sisters. He had brought his pupils down from St Andrews in Scotland to the family house, built by his grandfather, with many acres of land, ideal for playing fields. This land was mostly sold and built upon during the 1950s, so that most of West Horsham is now on it, and the school became a girls' school until its final demise in 1988.

Later, David also won a scholarship to Brighton College. Having both boys there was very handy for my parents, because they never had a car (apart from one which was given to them for a wedding present in 1916 and promptly sold to pay my father's Mess bills). The boys were allowed to come home on bikes every Sunday after Chapel. There was none of the performance which takes place now, when parents drive miles to collect their offspring from school. Quite often we went by bus to attend the Sunday morning service in the school chapel and hear John reading the lesson.

For the time being, David came home for the holidays from Horsham by train to Hove station, which was within walking distance of our house (although I must say we walked a lot further than children do nowadays). Being a great train enthusiast, he used to spend many happy hours during the holidays standing on the bridge at Hove station, watching the trains go under it. Sometimes I was privileged to be taken too, although he was inclined to bump into friends and forget about me. Once, he left me outside Hove Town Hall, but I knew the way to our house from there, and was able to walk home, getting some stranger to see me across the road. This would be dangerous nowadays, but you could trust people then.

With both boys away at school, life for me before I, too, could go to school was rather solitary. A great deal of my time was spent in the kitchen, which was down a dark, uncarpeted flight of stairs in the basement. I used to negotiate those stairs backwards, as there was a perilous twist at the top. The kitchen had one of those lifts on which the food was placed and then the whole contraption was hauled up to the dining-room by ropes. There were various bells in the upstairs rooms with brass and china handles. When, requiring a meal to be sent up, you pressed the handle down and then let go, causing a 'clang-clang-clang' to reverberate through the house, and there was a glass-framed board high up on the kitchen wall, with numbers on it to show in which room the bell was being rung.

In our poverty-stricken state you may well ask *who replied* to this summons…? When we left Storrington we had brought with us a girl of 13 called Virginia Greenfield, known as Jinnie, who wore a blue overall and white cap and apron on weekdays and a very smart black overall with a frilled white pinafore and cap when serving tea in the drawing-room on Sundays. She also doubled up as a sort of nanny (and I do *not* mean grandmother) to me, giving me meals in the kitchen which I mostly refused to eat. I still have vivid recollections of a scene over some underdone scrambled egg, which I was forced to sit and look at for what seemed like several hours. Since I could not say "Virginia", I called her "The Linear" (so much simpler). She came from an enormous family which populated most of Storrington.

However, one day when Jinnie was about 15, she did not return from her day off, and we heard later that she had run away with a tramp. After this, there was no one to answer the bells except when my mother had a house full of people at Christmas or Easter, when she was allowed to 'borrow' Aunt Queenie's maids – but they always went back and sneaked on her. Although she had been given the house and all the furniture in it, she was apparently not allowed to *move* anything or rearrange it or, crime of all crimes, *get rid* of anything she didn't want … "Madam," quoth the Sneaks, "she's thrown out that lovely Aspidistra wot was in the hall."

Consequently, we grew up in rooms made dark and gloomy by overcrowded furniture and knick-knacks, all collectors' items now, but huge and hideous to us: cavernous wardrobes that several of us could hide in – just right for playing 'Sardines'; marvellous for accommodating all the clothes.

Our drawing-room, however, was a light, sunny room with two huge sash windows which opened high enough for us to step out on to a verandah which ran right along the back of the house and had a long flight of steps leading down to the garden, which had high walls on either side and an even higher wall at the end. In the drawing-room were gilt chairs with red velvet seats, a marble table with gilt legs, Ming vases, a chaise-longue, an old sofa, many carved occasional tables from India, small Chinese cabinets, a folding card-table, and a rosewood piano, round which we gathered every Sunday after tea to sing Sankey and Moody hymns while my mother played. *Shall We Gather at the River?* was our favourite.

The walls of this large room were covered with many watercolours, mostly of India, painted by a great-aunt. A Persian carpet covered the main part of the floor, but there were polished boards round the edge.

The contents of this room would probably fetch a small fortune if auctioned by Sotheby's today, but unfortunately, my penniless parents were quite oblivious of the fact that they were, you might say, sitting in a goldmine.

Once a week, on Wednesdays, this room was 'turned out' and its contents dusted and polished by someone called Dorothy Sayers who lived with her old mother in part of our basement. They paid us a rent of seven shillings and sixpence a week (37½ p) for one large room, a pantry and a lavatory. They used a tin bath in their room when they wanted total immersion; Dorothy took three hours to clean the drawing-room each week. She was also useful as a babysitter. I enjoyed being left with her, because she used to tell me what *school* was like, and I could not wait to go. She had obviously enjoyed her schooling.

After Jinnie's departure my life became even lonelier: it seemed to consist of making mud pies in the garden, and indeed this occupation has recurred with unrelenting regularity at intervals throughout my life. If my father was going to do some gardening, he always said, "I'm off to make mud pies." The only flowers that we seemed to have in that garden were Japanese Anemones and London Pride. The 'lawn', such as it was, was used by my brothers and their friends for endless games of cricket, although it was not nearly long enough and they broke the kitchen window about once a week.

A few steps led down from the garden to the scullery door, and from there you went into the kitchen. I think my father did plant a few Hollyhocks against the end wall, but at this time his horticultural interest had waned and I gathered many years later that he was 'After Other Women' – two, at any rate, whom I called "Aunty Ruth and Aunt Elizabeth" … My mother was once heard drily remarking, "Those women are *not* your aunts …"

On Sundays John used to bring large numbers of school friends home to lunch, billiards, tea and Murder, in that order. The latter was a very favourite game: each player drew a card, whose identity they did not disclose, the lights were turned out, and the chap who had drawn the Ace of Spades had to 'murder' someone by putting his hands round their throat. The victim screamed – usually from genuine fright – and the lights were turned on. The 'detective' (prearranged and usually my mother) had to ask questions and try to guess who the murderer was. This was fairly easy, because the culprit could not stop grinning, or blushing.

'Sardines' was another popular game, although far more tame. One person hid while the others counted to 100; the first person to find him hid with him (or her) until everyone was squashed together (like sardines in a tin), leaving the last person to feel a bit of a fool when he found all the others together.

Being only four years old, I mostly just saw the long legs of the boys and not their faces, as I spent my time under the tea table, playing with their shoelaces. Sadly, many of these boys were destined to be killed in World War II; although far more of David's friends, now at prep-school, were to share this fate fighting the Japanese.

When I think of Hove, I remember the wonderful Christmases – all due to

David's ingenuity and technical ability, such as when he hired some children's films and a projector, made a beautiful screen with red curtains, and invited us all to a film-show in our darkened nursery.

I also remember my favourite walk, on which my long-suffering mother was frequently implored to take me to Davigdor Dairies, somewhere near Hove station, to watch the milk bottles go round on a conveyor-belt, first empty and then, magically, second time round, FULL! I was utterly fascinated … perhaps some child psychologist can tell me why.

Highlights in these pre-school years were visits from and to London Granny (Lady Pinhey), whom I remember as being quite tall, although I suppose it wasn't hard to look tall beside my mother, who was about five foot one. Granny's hair was rich brown and it never went grey. She wore long, flowing skirts with a long jacket, which must have been the fashion in the early thirties, and she always greeted me with a Hindustani expression that sounded like "Hullo Budmarsh" which Mr Patel in the corner shop tells me is Hindustani for 'naughty child' or rascal.

Sadly, by the time I was old enough to have a proper conversation with her, Granny was suffering from premature senile dementia – now known as Alzheimer's disease – brought on by a series of shocks which she had suffered, one after the other, in a short space of time. First, the sudden early death of her husband, then the loss of her eldest son, Kenneth, in World War I in the trenches, aged 21; and then I believe there was someone who wanted to marry her, but he died suddenly. (His name was Colonel Gimlette, which never struck me as funny, because I had heard it so often, but which caused one of my friends to explode with mirth when I was telling her this sad tale.) More tragedy was to come, which triggered off her illness. My mother used to say, "I wish you could have known Granny when she was at her best – so brilliant and amusing." Now I wish the same; my children hardly remember my mother.

However, for the present, Granny's visits meant a new winter coat for me, from Plummer Roddis in Brighton (now Debenhams) where I loved to go, because I was allowed to have a ride on a huge rocking horse which they kept in the middle of the children's clothes department.

Visits to Granny's London flat – in the Boltons – meant going to the Natural History Museum and the Zoo with Uncle Elliot … and that was always exciting. Elliot – we never called him "Uncle" – was Granny's fifth and youngest child. He was 17 years younger than my mother, born slightly prematurely when Granny was on holiday in Belgium (which has caused him endless trouble with passports) and always has been the most eccentric character in our family. He was named Elliot because his Godmother was Lady Minto, and Elliot was her family name. As his parents were in India, he spent a lot of time being brought up by Aunt Queenie, when he was not at school at Springfield and Clifton, and he also made frequent visits to us. He was only eight years older than my brother John.

When Granny had her London flat, Elliot lived there, working for exams. My mother said he took his School Certificate eight times and got it at the age of 21. This did not mean that he was a fool, but he was only interested in one subject, which was his life's obsession from the age of four: bugs, beetles, butterflies, moths and all insects fascinated him. He eventually became an entomologist of note, writing books on Rhodesian butterflies and moths and working as Curator of the National Museum in Bulawayo, until Independence and the advent of Zimbabwe forced him to return to England.

When Elliot came to stay with us in Hove my vivid memory is of the jellyfish: he brought special jars with him, and into these were packed the jellyfish which he collected carefully throughout his stay. I can still see the tall jars standing on his dressing-table, and these were taken back to London. I am not sure how Granny greeted their arrival. Her flat also contained row upon row of cabinets containing drawers of pinned specimens of butterflies, moths and beetles.

In 1938, at the time of 'The Crisis', Elliot was teaching at a school in Berlin. Then he came home and was smitten (not for the first time) with rheumatic fever. Somehow, during a spell in the nursing home at the top of our road, he got trapped into marriage with his night nurse, who was Roman Catholic. We all went to the wedding, during which the bride's sister sang *Oh, For the Wings of a Dove* and John muttered behind his hand that he felt sure Elliot was wishing for those wings at that moment …

The doctors had said that Elliot should not live in the damp English climate, so he and his bride departed to Southern Rhodesia, where he had been offered a j52ob.

This alliance did not last long, the bride returning shortly afterwards, having refused to consummate the marriage, which was later annulled. Eventually, Elliot found a marvellous wife, Nancy, who helped him with his work – photographs show her dutifully following in his wake, bearing a large butterfly net – and cared for him with unflagging patience. They had one daughter, Rosalind.

THE STUFFED STOAT

The best story of Elliot's eccentricity is a recent one. Every member of the Gordon family whose address could be found was summoned to attend a special service in St Paul's Cathedral to commemorate the centenary of General Gordon's death in Khartoum. This was a most impressive occasion, with beautiful music played by the band of the Royal Engineers, and a marvellous address on 'the life of Charlie Gordon' by a Senior Officer.

The Lord Mayor was there, accompanied by his wife, who, to my amazement, sported a head of shocking-pink hair … Even the Queen Mother had been invited, but had declined, characteristically pointing out that it would mean vast numbers of police having to be on duty on a Sunday.

Anyway, as this very moving service in the presence of all these august personages finally drew to a close, a different sort of whisper began to echo round the gallery: from pew to pew the whisper travelled – "Elliot's lost his false teeth; he thinks he may have dropped them into the collection …"

My imagination ran riot: were the choir standing round in the vestry at this very moment while the Dean of St Paul's tipped out the collection bag and revealed Elliot's gnashers? How embarrassing, and how had he come to do such a thing?

It transpired that he found it very difficult to sing with his teeth in, so during one of the hymns he had removed them, and had them in his hand when the collection was taken. He could not remember what had happened next, but he was no longer holding the teeth when the strains of the organ finally faded away.

John, who was more or less 'in charge' and had done most of the organising and laid the wreath, in his capacity as a recent Ambassador to the Sudan as well as being a great-great-nephew of General Gordon, was just about to suffer the ultimate embarrassment of having to ask the Powers That Were to tip out the collection, when, to everyone's relief, Elliot found the teeth in his pocket!

The South Africans and

Lord Hullin's Daughter

AFTER THAT 50-YEAR LEAP AHEAD, WE MUST return to the summer of 1934 when my mother told me that her sister, Aunt Molly, was coming home from South Africa with her husband, Uncle Staveley, and their two daughters, Pat and Rosemary, who were a year and two years older than I was (we were four, five and six). This was a great excitement for me, as they were very original and widely-travelled children, full of new games for me to play, very motherly with their dolls, and chatting endlessly about their voyage from Cape Town to Southampton.

Their father called them "Patty and Roey" in a strong South African accent. He was, in fact, their mother's first cousin, a Gordon, who had been brought up in South Africa and now served in the South African Mounted Police. He had amazing blue eyes and a pink face like a Dutch doll.

Aunt Molly was round and plump and had short grey hair, which surprised me, as it made her look older than I expected, in contrast with my mother, who was blonde, with long hair in 'shells' over her ears – very much a thirties' fashion – and when she had it cut short a few years later it went dark brown, but, like Granny, she never really went grey.

I missed my cousins when they went back to South Africa – but I was destined to see a lot more of them … unexpectedly soon. My most lingering memory of their visit was of getting into frightful trouble one afternoon when Pat decided that we would do some cooking in dolls' saucepans on a toy stove, and we grated coloured blackboard chalk and cooked it in water and then made up our faces with the resultant mess of pink, blue and green, smearing it all over our clothes and everything else in the room.

After the interlude with the 'South Africans', my next excitement was my first day at school. This I have never forgotten: every detail has remained a clear picture in my mind, and yet, at the time, my mother said I refused to tell her one word about it. The school was across the road and round the corner – only a few yards away. It was called Kenilworth House, but it had another house next to it, called Eaton House. One was for girls and the other for boys, but the kindergarten was mixed. There were just four of us, two boys and two girls. We sat on tiny chairs round a low table in front of the next class up, who all had desks.

The other girl was Jane Lane, whom I had already met at dancing-class in the Town Hall when we were three. Thin, pale and terribly delicate, her mother had died in India when she was born, and her father, Colonel Lane, who knew my father in the Army, had engaged a Norland nanny called Miss Hamilton (whom she called "Mummy") to bring her up.

Our birthdays were one day apart, so we had joint birthday parties, one year in my house and the next in hers. Poor Jane was to have a very short life, which ended when she was thrown from a horse at the age of 31, giving me a terrible shock when I read about it on the front page of the *Daily Mail*.

The two boys in the kindergarten were called George and Gordon. George wore a grey jersey and grey shorts which smelt of urine; this was the only thing I *did* tell my mother – in my own words: "George smelt like a lion" (a memory of those visits to the Zoo). Gordon wore a very shiny, dark blue jacket and shorts to match. He was not as aggressive as George, and had rather a weak face.

Mrs Wickham, the Headmaster's wife, started to teach us the alphabet, and we also did some adding with counters. However, when she found that I could already read (my father had taught me to read *The Tale of Tom Kitten* when I was four), she produced a book of poems for me to learn by heart. We all had to learn a lot of poetry, and when we were word-perfect we had the terrifying ordeal of reciting it to the Headmaster, of whom we were greatly in awe.

The rather unsuitable poem which was picked out for me to recite to him was *Lord Ullin's Daughter*, to which I insisted on adding an aitch, so that it came out as 'Lord Hullin's Daughter'. The poor man (the Headmaster, not Lord Ullin) must have had a job to keep a straight face at the sight of a small five-year-old solemnly declaiming in dreary tones: "One lovely arm stretched out for aid and one about her lover".

All this learning by heart was extremely good memory-training and I must say, most firmly, that I do not agree with the present thinking of the education 'experts' that learning by rote is bad. Once you have learnt something by heart it remains with you for ever – viz. Lord Ullin's Daughter, multiplication tables and history dates. How else would all my generation be able to calculate sums in their heads far more quickly than the calculators which children are so mistakenly allowed to use? If children were made to learn and recite poetry as we were, they would not have such appalling diction as they have now. Just listen to a young child or teenager being interviewed on television and you feel ashamed that anybody from another country should hear them and think that they were hearing correct English.

Why can't the English teach their children how to speak? It is inverted snobbery: they have this stupid idea that it is not fashionable to 'talk posh' – but why *have* a language if you are not going to pronounce it correctly? You would not deliberately sing a song out of tune!

It is a *very* different story when they learn a foreign language: tape recorders are used, great trouble is taken with pronunciation, they go on exchange visits abroad to perfect their accents – but they cannot speak their *own* language.

There was so little traffic in our road that I just used to run across the road and round the corner to school by myself. My favourite lesson was something called 'English Practice'. A pale green book full of sentences with blanks in them had to be copied out by the pupil, who had to insert the missing word, such as, 'The boys took off ____ coats' and you inserted the word 'their'; or 'The dog chewed __ bone' and you inserted 'its'. The sentences got progressively more difficult as the book went on, and we all worked at our own pace. I was fascinated, and loved the satisfaction of getting the right words to make the language flow.

Later, I was to go to a school where, I feel sure, English Grammar was taught more thoroughly than anywhere else in the world – and how I wish that every present-day television presenter could have been educated there!

KAFFIRS OR CAMELS?

ONE MORNING BEFORE SCHOOL I WENT INTO the dining-room and found my mother leaning against the sideboard, a letter in her hand, sobbing and being patted on the shoulder by one of the borrowed maids. "She was only 43," sobbed my mother.

Far away in a little village called Stutterheim, near Port Elizabeth in South Africa, Aunt Molly had died, giving birth to a son, who died with her. Uncle Staveley, broken-hearted, had written, on black-edged writing-paper, to break the sad news to my mother and to ask if she would bring up 'Patty' and 'Roey' if he brought them home to England. I don't think my mother even hesitated: small children were her life; she had helped to bring up her three younger brothers and now her sister's children needed her, so she would not fail them.

Not so my father: for weeks he muttered about 'kaffirs' arriving to invade our household. I wasn't sure what he meant when he kept telling me that "the kaffirs were coming" … The song, *The Campbells Are Coming* was popular at that time, and I thought it was 'Camels'; so between camels and kaffirs I became utterly confused, and nurtured a vague picture of black people with humps on their backs who were coming to live with us.

First, we took a trip to Granny's flat in London, so that my mother could break the news to her of the death of her eldest child. Seeing someone as old as Granny *crying* was a strange and new experience to a small child who had been told by her brothers that 'only babies cry', and the picture of Granny walking up and down her dining-room as my mother tried in vain to comfort her is one that has always stuck in my mind. Soon after this, Granny began to suffer from premature senile dementia, which was then described as 'a lost memory'.

The black-edged letters kept coming. Then, one cold, drizzly day, my mother took David to Southampton by train to meet Pat and Rosemary off the ship. They had been looked after on the voyage by one of their mother's friends, who was travelling to England and offered to help their grief-stricken father. I was taken to Hove station to meet them. They wore red coats with grey astrakhan collars, and they clutched teddy bears and dolls. Pat, who was now seven years old, seemed very grown-up and motherly to me, and was immediately very chatty.

From that moment I ceased to be the 'only daughter' and my solitary life changed for ever. Whenever we needed new clothes, my mother bought three of everything, so that we were always dressed alike. She was scrupulously fair, and no one could ever have accused her of favouring her own child. She must have longed to do so at times, but disciplined herself always to treat us equally as her three daughters. In fact, Pat, being the eldest, was slightly privileged.

Freud would probably have said that what came next was done on purpose by me, in an effort to make sure that I still got my mother's full attention; but, for whatever reason, from that time on I began to get illness after illness, spending weeks on end in bed, always feeling sick and not wanting to eat anything. So, not only did my mother have two extra children to look after, but she was constantly running up and down the stairs with medicines and meals on trays for me. How she found time, I don't know, but she always read favourite books to me, such as *The Wind In The Willows* and *The Secret Garden*, causing me to live in a dream-world as I lay in my bed, watching the cracks in the ceiling and turning them into imaginary animals and people.

Pat and Rosemary came to my school and were soon given important parts in the school play, *The Pied Piper of Hamelin*. I was the Chief Rat, which meant that I wore a grey outfit, more resembling a mouse than a rat, and had to lead all the other rats on to the stage.

It was after this that the illnesses really began: the school had an outbreak of measles. Somehow, Pat, Rosemary, David and I all got it at the same time, and our nursery was turned into a dormitory. The room was darkened and we were supplied with goggles to save our eyes from being affected. However, these precautions had no effect on me, and I have been short-sighted ever since.

Poor David suffered terribly – when he sat up, his nose bled, and when he lay down, he coughed. He was also very fed up at having to be in the same room as three *girls*.

When the others had returned to school, I got whooping cough, followed by bronchial pneumonia. It was thought that I was not going to live, and the crisis day was on my sixth birthday. My present was a dolls' pram, which was wheeled in and parked beside my bed. The red curtains were drawn, giving a pinkish light in the bedroom as the sun shone through the gaps.

Throughout that day I lay, immobile, hardly able to whisper, as anxious members of the family tiptoed in and out. That evening, the doctor ordered the nurse, who had been installed, to give me an 'egg-flip', which consisted of raw egg beaten up with sugar and brandy. Not many six-year-olds acquire a taste for brandy, but I did, and continued to ask for it, even after I had turned the corner and the danger had passed.

We had a marvellous family doctor with a lovely Scots voice, called Doctor Greig. He called every day and was a great comfort to my mother until he frightened her by telling her that I had caught pneumonia because she had not taken enough care to keep me warm. So remorseful was she that for the rest of her life, even after I was married, she fussed over me excessively, always pursuing me with coats and rugs to fling over my shoulders.

PAULEEN, THE ORANG-OUTANG AND THE CRISIS

BY THE TIME I WAS SEVEN YEARS old, the school round the corner was on the verge of bankruptcy and we were the last handful of pupils when it finally closed down.

We were then enrolled at Miss Rowntree's school, which was really called Westwood, and was on the second floor of a large building which also housed the Hove School of Music and William Willett's Estate Agents. My father nicknamed it "Cadbury College", but to most people it was just "Miss Rowntree's".

Miss Rowntree was tall, thin and ancient, with a neck like a foraging tortoise, which was shown to full disadvantage by her tightly scraped-back hairstyle which formed a meagre bun at the back of her neck. This was wont to come undone. While teaching, she usually stood with her back to a huge pair of curtains which divided her class – the top, naturally – from the next one down. One day, her bun came undone and wisps of grey hair protruded through the curtains, causing delighted giggles in the next room. Little things please little minds …

We had first heard of the school because my erstwhile enemy went there. Pauleen Lurcott had become my enemy at the age of five, when we had a punch-up in the public gardens on the seafront after she had called my father "a horrible old man".

He was very fond of small children, and used to buy bags of jelly sweets and hide them in the hedge and then invite all my friends to hunt for them, saying that the 'gnomes' had put them there. (He would probably be arrested if he did that now!) Most of my friends enjoyed the search – and the reward – but Pauleen, who was always immaculately dressed in white gaiters and had her hair curled nightly by her uniformed nanny, was 'Not Amused'. She had been told not to speak to strangers, and was therefore up in arms immediately, shrieking, "Go away, you horrible old man!" I launched myself upon her (although, even then, she was twice my height) and yelled, "My father *isn't* a horrible old man!" This, unbelievably, was the prelude to a close friendship which has endured for ever.

Miss Rowntree had a brother who came each week to give us Natural History lectures. We learned about mammals, reptiles, fish, insects, etc.

Rather revolting pictures of these were pinned to the blackboard and we had to copy them and write notes. *His* favourite – and ours – seemed to be the Orang-Outang. We all loved saying this new word, and Pauleen in particular was utterly fascinated. We decided that Mr Rowntree himself looked exactly like the Orang-Outang, and this became his nickname.

Miss Rowntree and my mother clashed violently over school uniform: there was no way my mother could afford three sets of pale blue everything, and she proposed to send us to school wearing our old uniform from the last school underneath light blue cotton overalls from Marks & Spencer.

In vain did Miss Rowntree send notes and messages of complaint. Finally, my mother arrived at the school to confront Miss Rowntree – and returned home victorious! For, as she arrived, Pat burst into the cloakroom, her nose streaming with blood (just a nose-bleed, not a fight) and I staggered out, ashen-faced, having been sick. "Now do you see why I send them in overalls?" quoth my mother triumphantly. Game, set and match, and we never wore the proper uniform, of which the blazer alone cost more than she would have had for a month's housekeeping.

Bearing in mind that I was seven years old at that time, and that recently there has been much political argument about the education of seven-year-olds, there were two subjects which were simply but excellently taught at Miss Rowntree's, in a way which was memorable for the rest of one's life, and these were Geography and French. A huge map of the world was pinned to the wall, a long stick, or 'pointer' was provided, and each child stepped up in turn and was ordered to point to France, Germany, or whatever, until gradually the position of each country, its capital, main rivers, mountains, etc., was firmly recorded in one's photographic memory. Why this is considered a bad way of teaching today, I can't imagine. Recently, a member of the younger generation remarked that she thought it very odd ... Why odd?

We had two French lessons a week: one, purely for vocabulary, was similar to the geography lesson. A huge, brightly-coloured picture of a farm-yard full of activity, with people, animals and farm implements intermingled, was pinned to the wall. Again, each child went up and pointed to something in the picture, saying the French word for it, if known, otherwise being told what it was, until we all knew the name of every single item in the picture, including the sky, the clouds and the earth.

The other French lesson was exciting, as we *acted* it. All the chairs were put in a long line and we pretended we were on a train journey: first, we bought our tickets (for a long time I was puzzled by something which sounded like 'Allyair-retaw' until I saw it written some years later – *'aller et retour'*, meaning a return ticket; literally 'go and come back'), then we sat in our seats and ordered refreshments. A dolls' tea set was carried along the line of chairs and we all had *'une tasse de thé'*. This was all completely oral, no written work, and we thought it a great joke and continued to use the expressions at home, which was good.

Unfortunately, before I started to enjoy these lessons, the change of school had an awful effect on me. Whether it was nerves, shyness with new children, or the aftermath of all my illnesses, I started being sick on every possible occasion, particularly when I had to go somewhere and face a lot of unknown children, such as a children's party. Going to the new school was agony: I felt sick – and *was* sick – every morning before school (like a permanent pregnancy). If I managed it before we left the house I was let off going. When my mother tried being hard-hearted and *made* me go, I used to be sick during the first hour (usually during prayers, into the white linen cover which was stretched over each cane chair at which we knelt) and I was taken home, recovery taking place within the hour.

My anxious mother took me to see dear Doctor Greig, who pronounced that I was fit and 'shamming' – but I really *did* feel sick. Perhaps I just wanted my mother's undivided attention, which I was never going to get as long as my cousins remained with us, which was for ever. Whatever it was, I continued to feel sick before any new experience, particularly social events, and right up to the time that I had children of my own.

One party that I really did enjoy, however, was the dreaded Pauleen's eighth birthday party, and this was the point at which hostilities ceased between us. I suppose I was invited, despite our state of Cold War, because the whole form was invited, and she couldn't very well leave me out.

My mother always took great trouble over getting the right present for the right person. We had a craze for pet tortoises at that time, and when Pauleen invited me to the party, my mother took me round to her house after tea one day to ask whether Pauleen would be allowed to have a tortoise for her birthday. Our mothers 'clicked' immediately and became great friends for ever. Pauleen showed me round her garden (near the sea and much prettier than ours) and we never fought again. I should explain that her name was spelt in this unusual way because her father's name was Paul and her mother's was Aileen (pronounced Eileen).

It became a habit for both our families to meet for tea on the beach almost every day. Mrs Lurcott's huge black-and-orange striped umbrella was a landmark on Woolgar's beach, which made it easy for us to find her. Every beach bore the name of the man who rented it annually to keep his boats on, which he hired out, and provided a lifeguard who was on the look-out for swimmers in difficulties. Until we joined the Lurcott family for tea, we had always gone to Hatton's beach, a bit further west. Mr Hatton was extremely fat and had several bronzed and handsome sons.

At the top of each beach was a kiosk selling ice creams (cornets at a penny and two pence each) and newspapers. I became fascinated by newspapers at an early age. The first exciting, all-absorbing news item that I remember was the story of King Edward VIII and Mrs Simpson. Pat first drew our attention to it when she arrived home from school saying, "Miss Rowntree says that the King wants to marry a *false wife* and Mr Baldwin won't let him!" She then cut out a huge picture of Mrs Simpson from the *Daily Mirror*, purloined from Dorothy Sayers, and painted it all the nastiest colours she could think of – green mouth, purple cheeks, etc.

In the summer of 1938 the newspapers were much in demand, owing to the threat of war, which seemed a certainty, and was referred to as 'The Crisis'. We children hadn't the faintest idea what 'crisis' meant, but our mothers were constantly sending us up to the kiosk for the latest edition.

I was inspired to produce my own newspaper: it was a very unofficial school magazine, called *The Rowntree Rag*. John, now at Oxford, demanded that copies be sent to him regularly. I still have one or two of these. On the front cover of one is a drawing of Miss Rowntree and the pupils devoutly engrossed in morning prayers, Miss Rowntree's nose touching the top of her desk, her head bent in reverence. Inside are advertisements for a badly-drawn blackout torch; stop-press news that 'Freddie saw a mine on the beach'; a picture of Miss Eldridge (the second mistress) in bed with flu, a very prominent chamber-pot under the bed; and Miss Rowntree driving 'an airaplane'.

Pauleen, not to be outdone, produced a rival paper, called *The Skool Screamer*, which, sharply in contrast with my chaste front cover, had, as its cover girl, Miss Rowntree sitting on a bright green lavatory. Her father promptly banned it.

Goodbye to Granny – and to Peace

Also in 1938 came our first associations with the village of Ditchling, on the other side of the Downs, north of Brighton. Sadly, Granny died there, at the Retreat on Ditchling Common, a nursing home run by devoted and dedicated nuns, who seemed very impressed that 'such a great lady' had spent her last hours in their care. Granny had been very popular in India and was also known in London for all the work she did for Queen Alexandra's Rose Day, Earl Haig's Fund, Queen Charlotte's Ball and other charities.

In *The Times* Professor Robert Sencourt wrote:

'Some 20 to 25 years ago no Englishwoman was better known in the Indian States than Lady Pinhey. She had entertained King George V and Queen Mary, Lord Hardinge, Lord and Lady Willingdon; she visited Lord Kitchener in Cairo; and with each left the charm of a wit, a brilliance, a whimsicality which were all her own. Her father, Sir Harry Gordon, was a brother of the hero of China and Khartoum. Brought up in the fine conventions of Victorianism, she soon exchanged them for an originality which delighted everyone. For she had withal the same sparkling, lively ease, the same quickness of wit, the same sympathy which noted and remembered everything that mattered, and the Nizam (of Hyderabad – pronounced "Nizz-arm") delighted to do her honour.

After her husband's death at Hyderabad in 1916, she had to face the change from the most gorgeous Residency in India to life in a flat in South Kensington. But, again at the instance of Lord and Lady Willingdon, she took charge of the children of the Maharaja of Patiala and lived for some years an ample life with them at Sheen.

The greatest part of her interests was always in India, and from India she delighted to welcome friends. The old wit, courage and quickness never failed her. They were one with a deep sacramental Christianity she shared with Sir Alexander, and shone the more nobly through straitened circumstances and through trials. Her friends will long be grateful to her for all she taught them of the spirit of the Gordons.'

There was a big funeral, and she was buried in Hove Cemetery. We children, naturally, stayed at home, being introduced afterwards to heavily-veiled, black-clothed relations who came to our house for tea.

Our second, and happier, link with Ditchling came when my mother's first cousin, Rose Gordon, returned from India where she had been serving in Queen Alexandra's Indian Military Nursing Service (QAIMNS) and very generously offered to send Pat to boarding-school at Miss Dumbrell's, where she herself had been educated. 'Aunt Rose', as we called her, was as yet unmarried and assured my mother that she could afford to send Rosemary too, the following year.

Finally, in that same, eventful year came Mr Chamberlain, waving his piece of paper: 'Peace in our Time'. I remember standing outside a seafront hotel, watching such notable French leaders as Daladier and Gamelin coming out of an important meeting with their British counterparts, and being told, untruthfully, by Uncle Elliot that Hitler was also in there.

However, it seemed that no sooner had we finished rejoicing that there would be no war after all, than the sandbags appeared outside the Town Hall, our parents became ARP Wardens, gas masks were issued, all windows were covered with criss-cross strips of sticky brown paper to counteract blast (I don't know how effective they were) and food rationing began.

Hitler's hysterical speeches made us shriek with laughter as we hung over our crackling wireless set – a huge, polished wood affair, which was the first that we had ever seen, and cost three shillings (15p) a week to hire – but little did we realise that it would be no laughing matter when the war really started and the air-raids began …

PART 2:

THE STUFFED STOAT:
AN EXCELLENT EDUCATION

PROLOGUE: 1938

IN 1938 OUR FAMILY HAD ITS FIRST close connections with Ditchling, when my cousin, Patricia Gordon, was sent to school at North End House, or 'Dumbrells' as it was generally known, and our grandmother, Lady Pinhey, spent her last days at the Retreat on Ditchling Common, dying there in June of that year, completing the link between India and Ditchling.

Many people say that they can remember exactly where they were and what they were doing on the 3rd of September, 1939, and I am no exception. We had spent a short holiday in Ditchling, where my cousins were at boarding-school and, because of the threat of imminent war, the two Headmistresses, the Misses Dumbrell, had invited us all, including my teenage brother David, to stay at the school for a week or two before the term started, while my mother returned to Hove to attend to such matters as blackout curtains, gas masks, sticky tape on the windows of our house, etc. Thus it was that we happened to be in Ditchling Church, accompanied by Mademoiselle Favre, the French mistress, at 11 a.m. at the moment when War was declared. Mademoiselle was in tears at the thought that she would not see her 'belle France' for several years perhaps, although foolish optimists were predicting that "it would all be over by Christmas".

Shortly after the declaration of war, or almost simultaneously as I recall, the siren sounded as a plane came over. That eerie wail of the siren was to strike terror into my heart for the next six years.

Fifty years later, I learned that the said plane, which everyone said was German, was in fact the light plane of Sir Stephen Demetriadi's son, trying to land on the Downs near his house, half-way between Westmeston and Plumpton.

However, on that fateful morning we were hurried back to North End House, half expecting to be bombed.

School is a subject which arouses in most people a stream of memories, good to some, extremely painful to others. These are usually sparked off by familiar smells, sights and sometimes tastes (such as bread pudding). I felt I had to write this account to make sure that Dumbrells' School went down in History, because, unfortunately for posterity, there will never again be a school like it, and there will probably never again be such remarkable and dedicated characters as the Dumbrell sisters and Miss Knowles, who devoted their lives to teaching just a few of us, out of four generations, to have not only an erudite and resourceful outlook on life, but a compassionate manner towards our fellow beings, at the same time saving us from being priggish goody-goodies by their delightful sense of humour, which they passed on to us. They were unique women, but would never have thought so themselves.

The quaint, timeless quality of the school has been its greatest characteristic, and it is interesting that pupils who left fairly recently have many similar memories to those of old girls whose memories go back 60 years. Its old-fashioned habits and customs may seem barely credible in 50 years' time: they hardly seemed credible 50 years ago, either.

Some will say that I have not written enough about the legends of past activities which were handed down – of girls cutting the hockey field with scissors, marking the hard tennis court with a toothbrush dipped in a bowl of white paint, and the circles on the netball court with a piece of string, a stick and a paintbrush; of sugar being locked in a safe every night during World War I; of a girl being expelled for winking at a choirboy in Church – and many other tales, but I felt that, for fear of inaccuracy, I should write only about the time which I had actually experienced, and as that time encompassed World War II, it was memorable.

How can any young person of the present day even begin to understand why, when schooldays are mentioned, I think with JOY of sitting on a fallen tree trunk, wearing a sun bonnet, struggling with algebra, in an orchard screened by dark pine trees, in which soldiers camped before D-Day?

North End House Home School, as it was originally called, was founded in 1882 by the three Misses Dumbrell – May, Edith and Mary – after the death of their father in a riding accident on the Downs. Their first pupils were young children whose parents were in India. Gradually, more pupils were taken in, of varying age, and boarding accommodation was added. The school expanded and flourished, surviving two world wars and maintaining its high standard of teaching right up to 1982.

Without doubt, North End, or Dumbrells, had a great influence on many people's lives, and now it was about to influence mine, for eternity.

1940 – "Take Me to Ditchling ..."

OWN IN THE BASEMENT OF OUR TALL Victorian house in Hove, my mother and I lay huddled together on a mattress. The air-raid siren had sounded, and so had some not-too-distant thuds of bombs being dropped at the other end of Brighton. This was our first taste of an air-raid, and it made everyone think that Brighton was going to be a constant target, although, as it turned out later, after the first two or three raids the Germans hardly ever bombed Brighton again. Some people said that this was because so many German tourists (including Hitler) had such pleasant memories of holidays in Brighton that they couldn't bear to destroy it.

However, on that first night, as we cowered in our kitchen, we felt that we were in great danger and must get away to the country. My mother had had no experience of raids in World War I, as she had been in India.

No thoughts of bravery entered my head; I was a thoroughly nervous and cowardly child, and I could not bear loud noises. On Guy Fawkes Night I hated the fireworks so much that I used to spend the evening under the sofa with the cat, while the rest of my family were enjoying themselves hugely, letting off rockets and Catherine-wheels at the end of the garden. Now, therefore, I had no compunction in screaming, "Take me to Ditchling – *please* – take me to Ditchling, *tomorrow* ..."

Ditchling was a safe refuge to me. It was a beautiful little village, nestling under the shelter of the South Downs on the inner side, away from the coast and about 10 miles behind Brighton.

It was where my cousins, Pat and Rosemary Gordon, went to school, kindly paid for by a cousin, Rose Gordon, who had been a pupil there herself and was as yet unmarried. I was very envious of their chance to go to boarding-school, and this was where I now wanted to be.

North End House was no ordinary school; in fact, there never has been and never will be anything like it. All the horrors of the outside world were left behind when you stepped inside the square hall with its cool tiled floor, stuffed animals in glass cases on the walls and a highly-polished staircase twisting back and up to the wide, shiny landing. It was a place where Time had stood still for 100 years, and it is impossible to explain to anyone who didn't go there how we came to love every moment spent in such old-fashioned, unworldly surroundings. Even in our time it was a legend and an affectionate joke, but to our friends and relations who went to normal, up-to-date establishments, such as Roedean and Sherborne, it was incomprehensible … they were the losers.

This did not mean that the education was behind the times – great care was taken to keep abreast of the academic standards of the day, and indeed we were kept above average in all educational requirements, and examination results were high. No one was even allowed to enter for School Certificate unless they were almost certain of matriculating on it.

This meant getting a minimum of five credits (Grade B nowadays) of which English Language, Maths and Science or Latin were compulsory. It exempted you from having to take a separate matriculation exam, which got you a university entry.

The school was often just referred to as 'Dumbrells', although its official title was 'North End House Home School'. ('Home' referred to the fact that girls could stay there in the holidays if their parents were abroad.) Our grandmother, Lady Pinhey, used to recommend it to all her friends in India, because their daughters could be left there in the holidays as well as the term. There was a farm attached to the school, and fresh, bright orange butter and creamy milk were provided. None of those far-off mothers needed to worry about their daughters' health, although, as will be told, winter conditions were spartan beyond belief.

Granny was told about the Dumbrells by her great friends in India, the Goodenoughs, whose daughter, Angela, attended the school and rose to be Chief Wren during World War II, causing the Dumbrells to be proud of her. Another pupil, Janet Mostyn, also served in the Wrens.

Pat had told me fascinating stories of the fun they had at school, acting plays, having stories read to them and then dressing up and pretending to be the characters in the stories, going for nature walks 'down the back fields' behind the school, pooling all the sweets that they took back with them at the beginning of term and being given three sweets each after lunch every day, which meant that they might get extra-delicious ones that another girl had brought back, and not just their own, which always seemed more boring than someone else's.

I had been to watch the Christmas plays, including a 'shadow' play, acted behind a sheet, and I had met the fearsome Miss Knowles, of whom everyone seemed terrified, but who was quite kind to me, a mere visitor. She had joined the school at the age of 10, had been Head Girl in 1920, and after spending some time in France, where she became qualified to teach French in French schools (but never used this qualification) she returned to North End as Assistant Teacher in 1924 – and never left. Actually, we were never allowed to use the word 'teacher', which was considered uneducated; we always called them 'mistresses'.

Miss Helen Knowles played hockey for Wiltshire and, like Miss Mary Dumbrell, took a keen interest in botany and gardening. Her amazing stamina was probably due to her training when she was required to tend the children morning, noon and night, stopping only after tea to do her corrections. She had to sleep in the same room as the children and was often called to attend to a sick child in the night.

Being a sickly, cowardly, everlastingly-ill child, it had never struck me that I would get the chance actually to go to the school, but now events overtook us rapidly; with thoughts no longer of my being too delicate for boarding-school, but only of my immediate safety, my mother rang up the Dumbrells the very next morning after the air-raid (their telephone number was just 'Hassocks 24') and arranged for them to take me that afternoon.

No uniform was needed, for they had none. The only item of uniform that we ever had – and this was compulsory – was a floppy Sussex sun bonnet, worn by mistresses and pupils alike.

You took your half-yard of cotton print – perhaps to match one of your summer frocks – to someone in East End Lane called Ada Cave, tall and gaunt, and she made the bonnet for a shilling … (Roedean, Sherborne and the Rest of the World, please note that we loved them and would not have changed them for all your boaters).

We never had a car; my father had been given one for a wedding present in India in 1916, but it had been sold fairly smartly to pay his Mess bills. Ten miles in the bus seemed a long way to me. Inevitably, as was my wont, I was sick in the bus, and it was a white and woebegone creature who staggered into Dumbrells School, 10 days before the end of the summer term in 1940, to become the last boarder ever under the old regime.

THE BELL, THE CLUB AND THE IRON BAR

A MAID IN CAP AND APRON OVER BLUE overall beckoned us to an old wooden seat in the hall, facing a stuffed stoat in a glass case which appeared to be gazing in terror at a stuffed bat on the opposite wall, while she went to inform the Misses Dumbrell that we had arrived. The stoat was the first thing I noticed, and ever after, when I thought of the school building, I saw the hall and the occupants of the glass cases. By this time there were only two Dumbrell sisters left: Miss Edith, who was the official Headmistress because she was the eldest, and Miss Mary, who was the Second Head and taught the girls from the age of 13 upwards, preparing them for School Certificate. Miss Edith only taught music.

From the hall, which was paved with cool, patterned tiles, you stepped up a polished wooden step into the dining-room, where the two sisters, and Mademoiselle Favre when she wasn't doing anything else, spent much of their time. The drawing-room, filled with priceless, elegant furniture and ornaments, was at right-angles to the dining-room and was only used for extra-special guests, parents of prospective new pupils, and, above all, piano lessons. On this occasion, as they already knew my mother, we were taken into the dining-room. Characteristically, I tripped over the step as my new Headmistress advanced to shake hands.

Miss Edith was tall and thin, with a mass of white hair swept upwards and pinned above her long face. My mother called her "the pretty one". When she smiled she did have a pale pink, pretty face, but like a lot of painfully shy people, she tended to look rather severe when serious.

Miss Mary was a complete contrast: much shorter and stouter – like Pooh Bear, almost tubby – her hair in an untidy bun behind her round, humorous face. It would be unkind to say that she was 'the ugly one' – she had so much character, such a grasp of politics and worldly things, despite the sheltered life they led, and she frequently scandalised Miss Edith by uttering extremely original, forthright remarks. Her utterances were rendered more humorous by an unfortunate affliction which caused her to sound as if she had a permanent bad cold. This, we were told, was *not* adenoids, but something more obscure, also beginning with 'A'.

The Stuffed Stoat

Miss Edith was dressed in blue, and Miss Mary in grey, and these respective colours were more or less consistent throughout my schooldays (and probably everyone else's). Their garments appeared to flow down to their ankles, without one noticing the exact details of what they were wearing.

Mademoiselle was smaller, with twinkly brown eyes under long, dark lashes, set in a rather plain face with a heavy jaw. On reflection now, I think that with modern make-up, she could have been rather attractive. Make-up, however, was a Dirty Word in those days, and to a small child she appeared rather grim and severe. The severity was, in fact, sadness, as she had no news of any of her relations and had been in floods of tears the day France fell to the Germans. Her clothes were typically French; always something pretty at the neck, an unusual collar or a little brooch, and a cardigan knitted by herself in an unusual stitch. When I arrived, Mademoiselle had already been at the school for 40 years, but she never lost her strong French accent.

The Dumbrells were inclined to treat Mademoiselle as part of the furniture, and seemed to kick her around a bit – metaphorically, I hasten to add. She always sat at the head of the side table under the windows in the dining-room, known as the 'French table', knitting incessantly, or, later in the war, reading the Free French newspaper. De Gaulle was the idol on whom all her hopes were pinned for the recovery of her beloved France.

If the Dumbrells didn't want her in the room, they got rid of her by sending her on some errand or other. On this occasion she was dispatched to take me and my suitcase up to the 'second east' room where I was to sleep with my two cousins. They did not call them dormitories, just bedrooms. There was the 'front room' where a lot of very small girls slept with one big girl in charge, two east-facing rooms, known as first and second east, and the landing room at the top of the stairs.

Various smaller rooms had to be approached by going through the Dumbrells' bedroom and up another flight of stairs. Some of the little ones actually slept in the dressing-room right next to the Dumbrells, so no nocturnal high jinks could be possible at all in any of those rooms.

The Dumbrells' bedroom was an absolute classic, more like 1840 than 1940. To enter it, you stepped down a steep step, landing on a small rug, which, if you were not expecting it, propelled you at speed to the far side of the room across the sloping, highly-polished floor. On regaining your balance, you turned to see a huge four-poster feather bed, in which the two sisters slept. Beside this on a stool near the door, stood a large handbell and a wooden club. For good measure, an iron bar was fixed to the back of the door, ready to be hooked across it to the wall. These three items were intended as protection against burglars (and rapists? I don't think they ever heard the word in their whole long, innocent lives).

All this Mademoiselle showed me, before unpacking my clothes. Then she led me downstairs again, through a dark passage past the pantry and into a small schoolroom, called the 'First' schoolroom; whether this was because it was the first one you came to, or because it was the first one they ever had, I was never too sure. The other classrooms had been added later, and were wooden with corrugated iron roofs (we were never in any doubt as to whether it was raining, as the noise on those roofs was more like the pitter-patter of giants than of tiny feet).

We passed through the first room, down two steps, and into Miss Knowles's schoolroom (funnily enough, we always called them 'schoolrooms' and not classrooms). This was also the gymnasium, with ropes coiled up near the ceiling, wall-bars behind Miss Knowles's desk, and fittings for parallel bars at the sides of the room.

I think of it now as a pleasant, rich brown, polished room with a warm atmosphere. Even the ceiling was wooden. It was to be the room in which I learned almost everything academic that I know, and in which Miss Knowles, perhaps unwittingly, cultivated my sense of humour by making me laugh at her brilliantly expressed sense of the ridiculous.

THE 'OGRESS'

AT THAT MOMENT, HOWEVER, BEARING IN MIND Miss Knowles's reputation for being a terrifying ogress, I was shaking with fright and sick with embarrassment when she and all the children looked up as we entered the room.

Miss Knowles glared at the interruption. I think she used to glare to allow time to collect herself to talk to strangers or other adults, for she was a very shy person, completely dedicated to her teaching. She had rather a red face, huge sea-blue eyes and wavy chestnut hair, stuffed into an untidy bun at the nape of her neck. Taken under Helena Rubenstein's wing, she could have been a raving beauty, but she just didn't care. She had grown up as a tomboy with two brothers, and never took any interest in men, although one or two proposals had been relayed to her via Miss Edith. She always wore the same clothes: a dark blue frock with a deep V-neck bordered by a cream-coloured collar, covered by a dark blue blazer when cold. Black stockings and very neat little plain black court shoes completed the outfit. Her feet were only size three. Years later, she told me that an aunt had left her 29 pairs of stockings and umpteen dark blue frocks, and being hard up, she had felt obliged to wear them, to save money.

The fact that Miss Knowles always wore the same clothes made her, as she herself said, "a symbol of stability" to us, her pupils, and it has been comforting in this much-too-rapidly-changing world to be able to visit the school and find that Miss Knowles still looked the same.

"Patricia," she commanded fiercely, "come and take your cousin to sit beside you while I finish the story."

Pat came out from her desk, looking demure with her hair in pigtails, and proudly took me by the hand – she was always very motherly – and squeezed me in beside her while Miss Knowles continued to read *Ivanhoe* in a very pleasant voice which held your attention and fired your imagination, as she was good at impersonating the various characters in the story. She had an amazing knack of appearing to be completely absorbed and yet being totally aware of what her audience was up to: for instance, she would suddenly break off and make us all jump by shouting, "Margaret!" (or whoever) "Bring that ink-well here at once!" (No one had biros then, and we dipped pens with detachable nibs into china inkwells which were sunken into little holes on the right-hand side of the desks.) The scarlet-faced culprit would produce an inkwell into which she had been stuffing blotting-paper to amuse herself while listening to the story. Somehow, Miss Knowles had managed to observe this activity.

I sat very still, as I had been told that Miss Knowles threw pencils and books at pupils who misbehaved or who couldn't answer her questions. Her word was LAW and no one would ever dare to question it. What a pity the present-day members of the teaching profession could not use her disciplinary expertise without fear of being taken to court by the parents. No schoolroom in the country was so well-disciplined.

While she read, the girls were pressing wild flowers, drawing and painting them and writing the names and characteristics of the flowers in exercise books with alternate pages of drawing paper between the lined pages: it was Miss Mary's greatest interest. There were frequent nature walks, during which you were expected to notice and pick as many different varieties of wild flower as possible – but not the rare orchids – and bring them back to be identified, either by Miss Mary, who was an expert, or by tracing their characteristics in a book called a 'Flora'. (Knowing how to use a Flora was an official requirement for the School Certificate Botany exam.) Then they were pressed, drawn, painted and noted down. At the end of the term there was sometimes a prize for the girl with the best collection in her book.

When Miss Knowles came to the end of the chapter, we were sent outside to play before tea, and Pat introduced me to her great friend, Angela Giles, who was rather stout and had a long, solitary pigtail down her back. A motherly soul, with kind blue eyes, she was always marvellous with the little children, and it was she who slept in the front room and combed the small boarders' hair in the mornings.

Angela and Pat together put a wall of protection round me, revelling in having someone younger, much smaller and extremely nervous to look after.

Various nosy children who came up to stare at me were sent away and told to 'M Y O B' (Mind Your Own Business).

We played in a secret camp in the pinewood, until tea time – and tea was my first Big Ordeal. We filed into the dining room where I sat between my bodyguards at the huge mahogany dining-table.

The Dumbrells had a farm attached to the school grounds. They did not actually own it, as it was one of five farms which were run by a bailiff called Mr Turner, but the man who farmed it was a jolly, red-faced fellow called Mr Holman. Consequently, the school was supplied with thick, yellow, creamy milk and bright orange butter. The tea table was laden with plates of huge slices of bread-and-butter, also referred to as 'doorsteps'. I was told that I had to eat two doorsteps before I could have jam or cake, which was home-made fruit-cake. As the slices were approximately one-and-a-half inches thick, I never got to the jam, let alone the cake. Anyway, you didn't get butter under the jam; just jam alone. The two together were considered utterly decadent. This was a hangover from World War I, because, at that stage of World War II, the rationing had not really got organised, although our orange butter was soon removed from us when restrictions became more stringent.

I was rather puzzled when I noticed that here and there were girls lying full-length on their backs on the bare wooden floor, seemingly immobile. "What are they doing?" I asked Pat. "Tidy marks," she replied, briefly. For each bit of untidiness – an article of clothing left in the wrong place, a forgotten book, a missing hair ribbon – a girl had to lie on the floor for half an hour. Girls who had amassed several 'Tidy marks' could lie flat on their backs for anything up to two or three hours, while the rest of the school stumbled over them. (What an original idea; how I wish I could have imposed it on my family.)

After playing outside once more, and watching the 'big' girls playing tennis, which they did every evening in the summer term, we were called in and given a mug of cold milk and a slice of bread and dripping, and sent to bed at six o'clock. Even the Head Girl went to bed at eight o'clock. No wonder everyone looked so healthy …

Incredible as it may seem, there was only one bathroom in the house, and baths were organised so that each girl had one about twice a week, but these were usually rather cool. We did our 'strip-washing' in the mornings.

Lunching on Bébé Mort

At seven o'clock in the morning a grim-looking maid called Alice deposited a can of hot water outside each bedroom door, and we were supposed to share it between us, taking it in turns to strip-wash in an old-fashioned china basin with flowers on it, with a matching jug containing the cold water. (It seems incredible that these jugs and basins now fetch a fortune in antique shops.) We washed discreetly, hidden by pink 'modesty' screens which stood beside each bed. If you took too much water you were most unpopular, as the last girl got practically none.

After combing my hair vigorously – "if you don't, Miss Knowles will do it, and she PULLS" – I was dragged downstairs at top speed, and had hardly entered the dining-room before I was rammed down on to the floor by my neighbour, nearly cracking both knee-caps, because Miss Edith had started praying. Even the maids knelt in the doorway, having hastily deposited the dish of kedgeree on the hatch.

As far as I can remember, the prayers were the General Confession followed by the Collect for the day. These morning prayers were not entirely new to me, for my grandmother in Cheltenham followed the same procedure and we stayed with her quite frequently. In fact, most big houses held morning prayers, with the servants being compelled to attend.

The kedgeree was unusual and absolutely delicious; it wasn't the usual smoked fish type, but consisted of bacon and egg, chopped very small, with rice. We had it on Sundays and Wednesdays.

I was separated at last from my protectors and placed with children of my own age for the morning's lessons. My inability to do long division soon came to light, but my mathematical humiliation was counterbalanced by an inborn ability to spell. The latter part of the morning was sheer joy: a singing lesson, but no ordinary singing lesson. We sang verses from *The Flower Fairy* books, set to music. Although I had apparently been born tone-deaf, I had all these books at home, and knew the words by heart, so I stood, uplifting my tuneless voice in:

"I'm little white clover, kind and clean, Look at my three-fold leaves so green, Hark to the buzzing of hungry bees, Give us your honey, Clover, please …"

or,

"I am the English rose …"

until lunch-time, and lunch at North End was An Event. Not for us the ghastly, mannerless snatch and grab of the self-service meals that our children regrettably experience – we lived in the Gentle Age.

When the first gong sounded, beaten with great gusto by Alice in the front hall, we queued up to wash our hands in the two basins in the boot-room, and then, 10 minutes later, when Alice really worked herself up to a second frenzy of gong-bashing, we filed demurely into the dining-room.

We stood behind our chairs until Miss Edith had said Grace – "For what we are about to receive may the Lord make us truly thankful."

The huge main table in the centre of the room was the 'English' table, at which sat most of the younger children. Miss Edith sat at the far end and Miss Mary at the end near the door. There were always two meat dishes, one at each end of the table, presided over by Miss Edith and Miss Mary respectively. Miss Edith usually had the joint, because Miss Mary's sight wasn't too good for carving, so she always got the cottage pie – referred to as 'potato pie' – and later in the war the meat was replaced by minced carrot. There were also rissoles, stew, and meat roll or fish pie at Miss Mary's end. We always had the same dish on the same day of the week – we knew that on Mondays it would be roast beef at Miss Edith's end and cottage pie at Miss Mary's. There were always two puddings: Miss Mary had the suet – treacle on Monday, baked bread pudding on Tuesday, jam roly-poly on Wednesday, chocolate sponge on Thursday and ginger stodge on Friday with a rather repulsive white sauce – while Miss Edith daily dispensed milk pudding and stewed fruit.

Although it looked as if you had a choice, and each girl was asked what she would like, there was an unwritten law that you had to 'go in turns', i.e. choose alternately, otherwise (or otherwizz, as Miss Mary said) there would not be enough of one dish and the other would have been left uneaten.

Two people next to each other occasionally dared to ask for the same thing without actually getting shot, but if three chose the same pudding it raised a thunderous frown from Miss Edith, accompanied by a testy exclamation, and Martial Law was imposed, the offender blushing to the roots of her hair and being made to change to her most hated pudding. It was in this way that I eventually came to like rice pudding: when I was forced to have it one day I found that it was beautifully cooked and not so horrific as I thought. It was always accompanied by stewed fruit from the garden, which was excessively sour, but no one would have dared to ask for sugar.

Miss Knowles sat at the side of the English table, and her job was to serve the vegetables. Even if you detested a certain vegetable, you were made to have one spoonful of it, and because of this I learned to like all vegetables, as, here again, they were cooked to perfection.

Usually, the youngest or naughtiest child sat next to the corner, well disciplined and trapped between Miss Knowles and Miss Mary, who were at right-angles.

Conversation of interest about news and current events was usually introduced by Miss Mary, who liked to make sure that we were all well-informed about the world outside.

Being rather vague and absent-minded, she would sometimes start waffling on about someone she had met down in the village that morning before Miss Edith had started Grace, and she would get glared at and cut short in mid-sentence.

The older girls had to sit at the long, narrow 'French' table down the side of the room under the windows, and were expected to address at least a couple of sentences in French to Mademoiselle during the meal, besides asking for their food in French. Consequently, there was a rush to sit as near to Mademoiselle as possible, so that no one else could hear the halting French remarks that we were compelled, blushingly, to attempt. It could be very embarrassing if you '*se trouved*' yourself at the far end of the table and had to bellow at her, with all those at the English table splitting their sides at your '*fautes*'!

Translating the names of the puddings sometimes proved difficult: "*Pouding au lait, s'il vous plaît*" covered all varieties of milk pudding from rice to semolina or tapioca. There was one girl whose favourite pudding (unbelievably) was tapioca, and I took the utmost care to sit beside her, so that I would *never* have to eat it. *Pouding au citron, chocolat, gingembre*, etc., were quite simple, but Spotted Dick, College Pudding and Cabinet Pudding posed a few problems.

Roly-poly pudding with jam coming out of the ends was known in our family as 'Dead Baby' (an expression gleaned by my brothers from Brighton College) and one day my cousin Pat dared to ask for "*Du Bébé Mort*", much to the delight of those around her. This produced no reaction, and she was forced to amend it to "*Pouding à la Confiture*".

Very seldom were these meals anything other than delicious, but just occasionally the stews were rather disgusting, and some of us can remember harbouring gristle in our mouths all afternoon, too terrified to leave it or spit it out. If a child really wouldn't eat all her food, the plate was taken along to the Big Schoolroom, where the unfortunate offender was forced to finish it in front of everyone and under Miss Knowles's strict eye.

Second helpings were occasionally given, on a very arbitrary basis: 'Good' eaters were given more of the food they liked, which they might have gobbled up first, out of greed. 'Fussy' eaters, who had tackled their 'bête-noir' first and were feeling very relieved that it was finished, were then blessed with a second helping of it, for they had 'obviously liked it' … Leaving the worst to last would not have helped, either, for this was a sign of 'saving the best bits to the end'. How could you win? You couldn't.

Miss Knowles always chose milk pudding: it would have been talked about for days if she had changed her habit and chosen a suet pudding for a change.

It was all those little unchanging things that were the essence of North End; things that always remained the same made you feel so safe and secure – and stable … like the stoat in the hall, '*Mustela erminea stabilis*'.

How sad I feel when I think that my children have missed the quaint experience of these lunchtime exercises in good manners and unselfishness, for you sometimes needed to be unselfish by choosing the pudding that you didn't want, so that your neighbour could have the one that she liked best on her birthday … (Years later, my son told me how horrified he was when he went to Winchester – motto: 'Manners Makyth Man' – and found that the boys helped themselves to bacon and eggs in their fingers from a central dish in the middle of the table.)

At the end of lunch, when the last spoon and fork had been neatly laid down, we all stood while Miss Edith said, "For what we have received may the Lord make us truly thankful."

As the war continued and rationing became stricter, with our growing appetites we were going to be very thankful indeed for those splendid and unique lunches.

HITLER ENDS AN ERA

AFTER LUNCH WE ALL RUSHED OUT TO play organised – and sometimes disorganised – games on the hard tennis court or on one of the lawns. We played such games as 'Red Rover', 'Waves', 'French and English' – sort of party games, disciplined, but nevertheless giving us a chance to rush about and let off steam.

Poor Mademoiselle usually had to be in charge of us during this half-hour outside, and I can see her now, standing at one side of the tennis court, wearing hat, coat and mittens, knitting, knitting, endlessly, a long trail of wool leading to her coat pocket in which she kept her ball of wool with its hole down the middle which so fascinated us. Years later she taught us to wind it with a thumb down the middle to make the hole. Poor Mademoiselle, she tried in vain to discipline us, but no one ever took much notice of her as she shouted, "Aw, you English chillern!" when the noise became too great.

In we went to lessons again, some from visiting staff who came on certain afternoons to teach one particular subject, such as Latin, Science or Maths, but more often than not we had the much-looked-forward-to story which was read to us by Miss Knowles. We got ourselves so involved and so identified with these stories that, in our free time, we pretended to be the characters, and acted imaginary episodes of our own.

The books were usually by Dickens, Scott, R. L. Stevenson, or some less well-known author; books such as *Little King Richard*, *Stumps*, *The Little Duke* – nearly all with an historical flavour. Sometimes, for a change, Miss Knowles read *Narrative Poems* and *Longer Narrative Poems* and it was a marvellous way of teaching us to enjoy them. Now, when people say to me that they have never read Dickens, Scott and 'that boring lot', I think how much fun they have missed and how lucky we were to have Miss Knowles's inspired way of reading to bring them all to life for us. She read quite unemotionally but very accurately and clearly, and all the feeling was left to our imagination. She was blessed with a remarkable speaking voice; whether shouting orders, quietly explaining mathematical problems, whispering confidential secrets or reading aloud, she managed to maintain an unquestioned authority and command. I can still hear the sound of her voice intoning from a brilliant text-

48

book entitled *The Grammatical Kittens* – "A preposition is a word that comes before a noun – *to* the farmyard; *in* a basket; Mummy came *from* town."

Time passed as we followed this full and regular routine, and I gradually got used to the complete change in my life, and settled into the school ways, becoming less terrified, but still clinging to Pat for safety whenever possible.

We did not know it, but when the last day of term arrived, we had, sadly, reached the end of an era, for during the holidays, the Dumbrells decided that North End would no longer take boarders. With the threat of a German invasion and, if not that, the frequent air-raids, they felt that they were no longer young enough to take the responsibility of getting the girls down to the cellar at night, they could not tell parents that it was a safe area – far from it – and they did not have the means or the inclination to evacuate the whole school to the West Country or the Lake District, as did many other schools. Ditchling was their home, so they wisely decided that, for the duration of the war, North End would become a day school.

Dumbrells School

SCRAMBLED BLACKBERRY PIE

At home in Hove events had moved rapidly. My mother, still convinced that Brighton and Hove would be flattened by bombs, decided to look for a house in Ditchling, so that we could still go to North End as day-girls. Miss Mary Dumbrell persuaded a friend to let us rent a small cottage from him for £1 a week, and my mother found a tenant for our house in Hove who would pay her £1 a week. He planned to use the house as a furniture store for all the people who were abandoning their houses and fleeing to the West Country. This rent was not much for a house with three floors and a basement, but he stored all our furniture there as well, free of charge, except for a few things which we took to the 'semi-furnished' cottage.

Finding this cottage for us was just one more example of the essence of the Dumbrell sisters: their duties did not just end in the classroom; they did so many kindnesses to the parents and children *out* of school, and so much good to people in the village. They knitted jerseys and gloves for the poor families, and I am told that Miss Mary was Godmother to half the illegitimate ragamuffins in the area.

So, when the end of term came, we moved into No. 1 Hill's Cottages, East Gardens; a very humble domain. It was one of a pair of cottages with a large elm tree on a mound of grass just outside the gate.

To get to school we just had to walk a few yards up the lane to a stile, and through two fields, the second of which was our school hockey field.

My brother John had abandoned his degree course at Oxford and joined up in the Argyll and Sutherland Highlanders, with whom he was now serving in Palestine. He did not join the 'family' regiment – the Gordons – because they had rather a bad reputation at that time. I still have the two embroidered handkerchiefs which he bought for me in a little church in Bethlehem and sent home in a tobacco tin.

My second brother, David, had just left Brighton College and at 17 was too young to be called up, so he found a job in an office in Brighton, to which he rode on his bicycle eight miles over the Downs every morning. Being a born mimic, he regaled us every evening with hilarious imitations of the people in his office. He also joined the Home Guard and spent nights on Ditchling Common, watching for incendiaries, crashed planes and German pilots who had baled out. One night, he and an old man called Mike Marr had to run like hares to get away from a whistling bomb which was coming straight for them, and which landed on the railway line as they threw themselves flat on their faces.

My father also busied himself with the Home Guard, becoming Second-in-Command of the Ditchling Branch (he had been a Regular in the Indian Cavalry with the rank of Major) and travelled around giving lectures on strategy and tactics in surrounding villages, organising military exercises and doing the paperwork at HQ in the Beulah Chapel in East End Lane. Looking back and remembering odd incidents and conversations, I am sure that it was very, very like *Dad's Army* ... His 'boss' was a Major Wigney from Westmeston.

At about this time, Miss Edith received a letter from an Old Girl who had married a very rich man in South Africa. She had heard that shiploads of English children were to be evacuated to South Africa to stay with families over there for the duration of the war. She told Miss Edith that she would give a home to 'any two girls in the school who were a deserving case and would benefit from being educated free of charge, and had perhaps lost their parents ...' and so on. Miss Edith, knowing that Pat and Rosemary had been born in South Africa, that both their parents had died there and that my mother, with very little money, was going to have a struggle to bring up three of us in wartime, immediately contacted her, and the question was put gently to Pat and Rosemary, who were now aged 12 and 11 respectively.

Pat was reluctant to leave us, as she was devoted to my mother (whom she called 'Aunt Vi') but Rosemary was quite keen for the adventure.

They were given plenty of time to make up their minds, and in the end each said that she would go if the other would. They were to be escorted by a governess who was travelling out to Cape Town and would look after them on board ship. All the preparations, obtaining documents, waiting for a passage, etc., took a long time, during which my mother went through agonies of anxiety, wondering whether she was doing the right thing for them and thinking that if the ship were to be sunk, she would be responsible, etc., etc.

In the meantime, the Battle of Britain took place over our heads, literally. Throughout that long, hot summer the dog fights were carried on above us by day. At night my father used to walk up the lane and stand by the stile, looking across the fields at the sky over London, where he could see the searchlights and hear the barrage of the guns.

The Downs were out of bounds, as the anti-aircraft guns were up there:

huge, bulging tunnels of barbed wire fenced off large areas of countryside in case of invasion and also to keep the general public out of military camps. No more nature walks to look for Bee-orchids until after the war, and no more bathing on the beaches at Brighton and Hove, because the sea and the beaches were mined against the possible arrival of German ships.

However, we were still allowed to have picnics on Lodge Hill, a small, bracken-covered hill which was approached from a lane near Ditchling pond, and which commanded a magnificent view of the Downs and the Weald. This was our favourite place, where we could play hide-and-seek or tracking games in the bracken, following endless mysterious tracks made by rabbits, foxes and badgers, and climb the many small hazel trees, which were easy to climb but gave one such a sense of achievement and bravery on reaching the very top. We gorged ourselves on unripe nuts and wrecked our tummies. At other times we simply lay in the sun and gazed at the view. Alas – even up here there were slit trenches into which we occasionally threw ourselves if the siren went and we thought it safer to stay where we were than to try and get home.

I can remember lying on Lodge Hill, dreaming and studying the amazing variety of wild flowers in the small patch of grass by my finger tips: Hop Trefoil, Vetch, Creeping Jenny, Cinquefoil, to name but a few, with tiny insects running in and out and climbing up and down them as if they were in a large forest. It was strange to think that across the Channel, which was only the other side of the Downs, the Germans were oppressing country after country, men were fighting fierce battles, and everywhere in Europe there was terror and bloodshed.

One Sunday we were in the middle of lunch, and my mother was just getting the blackberry pie out of the oven (we had all picked the blackberries the day before) when we heard a buzzing noise. It got louder and louder until we realised that it was the sound of aeroplanes.

The next minute, four yellow planes flew past our windows a few feet from the ground. David rushed out of the side door, looking up and yelling, "They're Germans! They're Dorniers – get down!" We rushed into the passage which ran through the middle of the house and lay flat on our faces, our hands over our ears, as instructed by the ARP leaflets. The siren wailed – a bit late.

I shall never forget that moment. In retrospect I suppose they could not have been so low, but it seemed as if they passed at the level of the dining-room windows. Certainly that day a new word joined the current jargon of the day – 'hedge-hoppers' – the name given to enemy planes that flew low and machine-gunned the population. We could hear sounds of machine-gunning: "It's not safe here," said my mother. "Let's make a dash for the school and take shelter in their cellar."

We waited a few minutes until there was no sound of aircraft or gunfire, and then my mother picked up that blackberry pie in a cloth, said, "Quick now, follow me," and we all leaped over the stile at the top of the lane and ran, heads down, hell-for-leather across the two fields to the school, where my mother, still clutching the pie, described our sudden, frightening experience to the startled Dumbrells.

Not only did they have a cellar, but they had a passage in the oldest part of the house with walls four feet thick and no windows.

This was a safe place to stand during air-raids – and the entire school frequently stood there during the next few years. The kind old ladies said that we were welcome to take shelter in the school whenever we liked, and we finished our blackberry pie there as the All-Clear sounded …

On this Sunday afternoon we were not the only family who had a fright: the German planes had taken to hedge-hopping to lower the morale of the British people, and had been round the village, machine-gunning people's front doors and 'buzzing' houses (zooming down and coming up again at the last minute). Imaginations came into play as villagers tried to outdo each other with tales of their experiences, and one old woman said she "saw the German pilot pick up a bomb and throw it at her".

BRITISH JELLYHOOD

NIGHT RAIDS BEGAN IN EARNEST, AND WE took to sleeping on mattresses in the hall. These were rolled up and stood on end during the day, and, being utterly terrified, I used to climb down inside one whenever a Battle-of-Britain dog fight commenced. The rest of the family used to stand outside, calmly watching the fight-to-the-death in the sky, but I remained inside my mattress with eyes closed, moaning at intervals as if in child birth, waiting for the certain annihilation which I expected. My mother, who had a great sense of humour, must have written to John about it, because she received a letter from him, "somewhere in the Middle East", asking, "And how is my sister, that quivering specimen of British Jellyhood?"

During one daylight raid we happened to be out for a walk about three miles from home, near the hamlet of Westmeston, which claims to have the smallest Church in Sussex (although I think that Coates, near Fittleworth, is smaller) when the siren wailed its dread warning. We were in quite open country, and the only thing to do was to knock on the door of the first house we came to, and ask if we could take shelter.

Rather a strange, wild-looking woman kindly let us in. Although she had no air-raid shelter as such, it was probably a relief to my mother just to be inside four walls with another adult to share her anxiety. Our hostess led us straight to her kitchen to see her cat's kittens, which certainly took our minds off the fighter planes doing battle overhead.

The mother cat was a beautiful Persian, and her children were adorable bundles of fluff. By the time we had been given tea and cake and my mother had discovered the amazing coincidence that the owner of the house was my father's C.O. at the Home Guard, the All-Clear had sounded and we were ready to go on our way, but now our family had increased by two, for we had been given the kittens. Panda, the boy, was black and white, and Puffball, his sister, was multi-coloured, not really tortoiseshell, or tabby, but a bit of both with white. This mixture made her one of the prettiest cats ever. We felt that, for once, Hitler had done us a good turn, for we would never have had those kittens if it hadn't been for the air-raid. I was to stand in many a queue at the fishmongers on their behalf, asking timidly for "a pennyworth of fish heads, or a penny herring"; for 3d you could get an enormous parcel of fish pieces.

We already had one cat at home: Patacake, who had moved with us from Hove. He was a large, dark-brown tabby with no white on him, and a black nose and lips. This is supposed to be much better in the cat world than having a pink nose and mouth, which is considered Rather Common. He was called Patacake because he used to sit in front of the fire, playing with his paws, putting one on top of the other, as in 'Patacake, Patacake, Baker's Man ...' Having ruled the roost as our only pet for two years, he did not greet the newcomers at all kindly, and spat nastily, but eventually the three of them settled down to an uneasy cold war.

Patacake had been 'arranged', but Panda never was, and he and his sister spent a happy, incestuous war producing 74 kittens over nine years. I do not say that she was always faithful to Panda – there were others in her life, who thronged our doorstep from time to time, and I do remember my father bellowing "Rahab!" at Puffball, although I had no idea what he meant. One of her lovers in particular was a disreputable, moth-eaten-looking creature, nicknamed 'Faithful and True' by my mother, because of his persistent devotion.

Term started again during the third week in September, when the Battle of Britain had reached its climax, and it was a much-depleted school that reassembled. Many of the visiting staff had gone to do war-work, and there were some new visiting staff to teach certain specialised subjects. Classes were rearranged a bit and were, of course, much smaller, which was a great advantage. It has been said that North End was like 'going to stay with favourite aunts in the country and having governesses', for we really did get individual attention.

If you fell behind in a subject, you were invited to stay for tea and be coached afterwards, so that any difficulties could be explained and you could be helped to catch up. No charge was ever made for this; money was never a barrier to anything.

Another activity which could bring us back after tea, if we lived near enough, was fruit picking. Cherriman, the Dumbrells' gardener, with his scarlet snub nose and whiskery face, reigned supreme outside, and if he decreed that the currants were ready to pick, then out came the whole school, usually after lunch, but sometimes after tea, to pick the red, black and even *white* currants for Cook to bottle or make into jam. Plums and apples were also in abundance.

Mr Cherriman was held up as an example to us all for his stolid way of working slowly and doggedly from dawn to dusk. "A good gardener never hurries," quoth Miss Knowles, as we tended our own individual plots of garden near the hard tennis court.

I Join the Axis Powers

Shortly after the term began, Pat and Rosemary's departure date was fixed and they were taken to London to catch a boat train from Euston. Many weeks later we received a marvellous letter from Pat (aged 12) describing how there had been an air-raid and they had had to spend a night in the underground and had many adventures just getting to the ship, let alone the hairy voyage in convoy to Cape Town. Her letter gave every detail of all that had happened from the moment that my mother handed them over to the governess who was taking care of them throughout the journey.

So, I was left alone at school to battle with the appalling shyness which never really left me until I was well into my twenties. Gradually I made friends with the other children, tending always to mix with children a couple of years younger than myself. After all the childhood illnesses which had assailed me in my earlier years, the doctor said that I would be two years behind in physical growth and development.

My first friend was Sam Adshead, a highly intelligent, extremely eccentric and delicate boy with much the same history of illnesses as myself. He was eight years old and would soon be going to prep-school. His father was a Naval officer who died quite early in the war.

Another little friend was Margaret Fox, with a sweet face and fair hair in an Eton crop (her father was longing for a son). She used to call for me on her way to school each morning so that we could run through the fields together. Her parents had also been in India, and soon made friends with mine. She was eight years old but extremely self-possessed, and I followed her lead in everything, although I was 10. She was the eldest of her family; I was the youngest of mine. Throughout life I have found that where you come in the family makes a tremendous difference. Being the youngest means that you always expect other people to take the lead, whereas people who are the eldest automatically boss others about. Children in the middle tend to be the nicest.

One day, Sam had the wild notion that he and Margaret and I should call ourselves the Axis Powers: he would be Hitler, Margaret would be Mussolini and I, with my round face and black hair, would represent Japan. (I was not too pleased about this, and anyone less like Mussolini than Margaret would be hard to imagine, but we decided that it was good for a laugh – and Margaret was one of those people who always had to be in a gang.)

Sam, however, entered into the spirit of it so seriously that he almost *became* Hitler; ranting and raving in 'pretend' German and not letting any of the other children near him.

When we had team games we made sure that the Axis Powers were in the same team. Inevitably this charade was not allowed to continue for long; Mademoiselle was horrified, and sneaked on us. We were given a lecture on our lack of patriotism, and the Axis Powers were disbanded forthwith.

All through that autumn and winter the air-raids were going on; we seldom slept upstairs in our beds, but always on mattresses in the hall, with all the doors shut to avoid the possibility of flying glass from the windows in the various rooms. One night, Major Wigney's front door was blown straight in, through his hall and out through the back door.

There were bomb craters to be seen in the fields, where the Germans had jettisoned remaining bombs on their way back from London after being chased away by our fighters. Sometimes we collected pieces of crashed German planes. One girl at school showed off a piece of the plane that bombed Buckingham Palace and was shot down, which her father had brought her from London.

The trunk of the elm tree outside our gate was riddled with bullet holes from low-flying machine-gunners. One morning, Margaret and I were half-way through the fields en route to school when we heard a low droning sound and saw German planes approaching at tree level. We flung ourselves face downward in the ditch until they had gone over, and then made a dash for school, but had to repeat the performance by diving into another ditch before getting there.

During some of the daylight raids we all got under our desks, Miss Knowles continuing to read to us from under *her* desk, causing a few giggles, which did relieve the tension. There was one girl who was even more nervous than I was – she used to have hysterics and shake and scream – and this made me feel better. At least I kept silent – paralysed with fear …

When we heard bombs dropping and anti-aircraft guns firing, we used to be taken down to the cellar, which was about six inches deep in water. There we would stand and recite our multiplication tables, or have mental arithmetic. At other times we would squeeze into the passage outside the kitchen, in the oldest part of the house, where the walls were four feet thick.

'Aunt' (really cousin) Rose Gordon stayed with us quite often at that time, because she was nursing at Netley Hospital, just outside Southampton, which was very badly bombed. In the middle of it all she managed to catch mumps, and sent me a funny poem about it, with illustrations. She was a clever artist and wrote a book called *Sicknesses of Josephine*, all in rhyme. It must have been the fashion for people to illustrate their letters at that time, for my father also used to do wonderful drawings all through his letters. Sadly, I no longer have any of them.

Letters from John were now few and far between, although he was a good letter-writer. He was fighting in the Western Desert under General Wavell, and was at the battle of Sidi Barrani and at Tobruk. Shortly after this he had to go to hospital in Alexandria to have his wisdom teeth out, and he felt so ashamed when Queen Mary was visiting the wounded there and he had to say that he was only having teeth out.

David was called up and went into the Royal Engineers through a special scheme whereby he went to Birmingham University for six months, so he was there during the worst raids.

Thus the war and my schooldays went hand in hand. We took far more interest in the news than present-day children, who tend to go out of the room as soon as the news begins. We hung round our crackling wireless set and also followed the progress or otherwise of our troops, shown by arrows on maps of battle-areas in the newspapers. There was a very good programme broadcast for schools, called *Current Affairs*, to which we listened and made notes.

The German invasion of Greece and Crete took place, and although we did not know until later, John's battalion was moved across from Egypt to Crete.

The first our parents knew of this was the telegram which all parents dreaded, saying that John was 'Missing'. My mother, naturally, was in despair; my father tried to be hopeful. So many of the boys' school friends had already gone down in ships, been shot down in the air, or killed at Dunkirk, and now the tragedy of war had hit our family.

"Goodbye Ditchling – Hallo Hassocks"

Now 11 years old, I carried on being absorbed in school life and my small band of friends, but was deeply hurt one day when I heard my mother tell Miss Knowles that I appeared to be utterly heartless as I was showing no emotion at all about John. Unlike the rest of us, my mother, apart from the chores and the daily conjuring with inadequate rations to produce adequate meals, had nothing to distract her from worrying incessantly. The fact was that every time I thought about John, I could see him in my mind, tossing about in a rowing boat on the sea somewhere. The picture was vivid, and I just knew that he was alive, but I could not bring myself to *say* this to anyone, and I couldn't explain it. It later transpired that this was exactly what he *was* doing. My mother was usually the one who was a bit 'fey', but at that time she was so wound up with anxiety that her psychic instincts did not come to the rescue.

John and a friend called Malcolm MacAlister Hall, having been captured at Crete and taken to Athens, subsequently escaped from the POW transit camp, lived with a Greek family for a while, and then decided that one of them should try to get across to Turkey in a boat and the other should try to get all the way round by land.

Thus it was that I had 'seen' John in a rowing boat. He was caught by the Luftwaffe and flung into the Avaroff public gaol in Athens for a fortnight until he managed to prove that, despite being disguised as a Greek peasant, he was, in fact, a British officer.

Long before we heard from the War Office, we got a long letter from John, postmarked 'Piraeus' and posted while on the run from the Germans. He had first been captured in Crete while riding

John Fleetwood Stewart Phillips. 2nd Lt Argyll & Sutherland Highlanders. Aged 21.

a motorbike inland with dispatches, not knowing that the British forces there had surrendered. He had been shot in the knee so that he came off the motorbike, had then continued on a mule, until it ran away, and had finally limped into a chemist's shop to get something for his knee, only to be confronted by two Germans with submachine guns. Since then he had managed to escape, and when he sent the letter, was on the run and living with a Greek family near Athens.

While on the run, John and Malcolm had many adventures, such as staying in a maternity home disguised as an expectant mother and her attendant – brandy was frequently called for when the expectant mother felt 'faint' – and on another occasion, hiding in a huge bakery amongst the loaves. It was a pity that he never, like many others, wrote a book about his experiences, but he probably preferred to forget them, for they can't have been too funny at the time. He was later sent to a POW camp at Lamsdorf on the border of Czechoslovakia (Stalag VIII-B) and eventually he went to Oflag IX-A near Kassel, in Germany.

We had many letters from Stalag VIII-B, telling us which friends were in the same camp with him, how he spent his days studying German, Urdu and Arabic (with books supplied by the Red Cross) and how he concentrated all his thoughts on preparing himself for a good job when the war was over. This was the best way to tackle the situation, to keep his mind on the future. He told us that he was hoping to move to Oflag IX-A, so it was no surprise to us when the War Office finally got around to notifying us that he had moved there. Official information filtered through War Office channels very slowly, so it took months before this happened, and John's own letters usually got through first. Only when my father applied officially through the Ditchling Home Guard did he receive a small scrap of paper stating John's final camp number.

Meanwhile, in Ditchling the sun always seemed to be shining, we had endless picnics on Lodge Hill, which was our favourite place, and I became very keen on tennis, gym and hockey, although I was not long enough in the leg to be very good at these sports. I was the same size as the seven-year-olds at school, so when the teams were being picked for hockey I was always left until last, because no one had noticed me standing there ... Before playing hockey, we all had to chase the sheep out of the field; our game was full of extra hazards as we slid about on the sheep droppings ...

I was thankful never to be chosen as centre-forward, because when we had matches against the evacuees they were such a bunch of toughs (boys included) from the East End of London, that our centre-forward usually ended up with a bloody nose.

We only had one 'big boy' at our school – most of them left at eight or nine and went to prep-school – but Brian Beer was the exception. He had been at a prep-school in Seaford, which was bombed. His parents decided to keep him, together with his sister, at day school, so they got special permission from the

Dumbrells for him to come to North End. He was a special friend of mine – six months younger than I was, but twice the size, of course – and I spent many happy afternoons playing in his garden at Wivelsfield and having tea there at weekends. His sister, Elizabeth, three years younger, was extremely good at art, and Brian was a great asset to our hockey team against the evacuees.

Although I was now more or less an only child, when I say 'we' had picnics I mean that my early friends from Hove visited us frequently. It was 10 minutes on the train from Brighton to Hassocks and about the same from Hassocks to Ditchling on the station bus, or they could come all the way on the Southdown bus, taking about half an hour.

I had also been permitted the great honour (by courtesy of Margaret Fox) of being allowed to join the 'Barnfield Gang', which consisted of all the children who lived in and around Barnfield Gardens.

We would meet on our bikes after tea, and drift into each other's houses (not mine, which was further away) and generally muck about. One afternoon I remember, we had a competition in Valerie Trent's house to see who could do the best imitation of a person we all knew: I got first prize (one of Valerie's books which she didn't want) for an irreverent imitation of Miss Mary Dumbrell. I kept that book, with its misspelt inscription, hastily scrawled by Valerie, for about 30 years until it vaguely disappeared in the mists of time and house-moving. It was about lace-making in Besançon (no wonder she didn't want it). Strange how these little facts stay in one's memory.

At the end of the summer of 1941 a blow fell when our landlord died, and we had to look for another cottage. We did not want to leave Ditchling, but in the end we had to, as the only house we could find to rent was in Hassocks, three miles away. This was a very modern, semi-detached house on a huge estate, originally called 'The Hassocks Homes' but later given the rather pretentious title of 'Grand Avenue'.

The kitchen was full of gadgets: everything folded neatly away into a cupboard – the kitchen table and the ironing board just disappeared at the press of a button when you wanted to clean the floor. We had a lawn with flower-beds and a vegetable garden through an archway of roses beyond the lawn.

In a way, the new house was more convenient, as we were able to walk to the station, but my father had to catch a bus to the pub every evening (he refused to abandon the North Star at Ditchling).

I alternated between riding a bike three miles to school, walking through the fields, my route coming out opposite the school, when the weather was too icy or snowy to ride the bike, and taking the bus – for 1½d – on wet days.

Saturdays, however, were bliss. Ten minutes on the train from Hassocks and we were in Brighton, where one could browse through the second-hand bookshops in the Lanes, where first editions of old historical novels were to be found for a shilling or two and stamp-shops were a paradise to the collector.

Lunch for 1/9d in a blue-painted coffee-shop, followed by a film, and then home again on the train, made a really happy Saturday; our pleasures were simple and discos were unheard of.

At the end of our road in Hassocks was a cinema, to which we went about twice a week (at a cost of 9d for children and 1/3d for adults). My mother simply loved the cinema and it was our great treat in those pre-television days. When David came on leave he also came with us, although my father never did. The only time I remember him going was when I was three years old and he took me to see a Laurel and Hardy film in which one of them swallowed a feather from his pillow and it blew out of the other one's mouth; I never forgot it.

As I grew older I really looked forward to David's leaves, and the eight-year gap between us began to diminish as I enjoyed his company and appreciated his humour more and more. One film that we went to see had us in stitches, as it was the first time we had seen the 'Boogie-Woogie' being danced. My mother thought it rather vulgar, but when we got home David taught me to do it in our small dining-room until we were giggling helplessly.

David progressed from Birmingham University to a training camp at Ripon in Yorkshire, from which he wrote cheerfully and regularly every few days, telling our mother every detail of his army life, into which he settled with great enthusiasm. He always sent messages to his old pals in the 'North Star', with whom he had served in the Ditchling Home Guard. We kept every one of his letters, which are now a marvellous record of the life of a soldier at that time. From Ripon he went to an OCTU at Beaumont Barracks, Aldershot, from which he was able to get the odd weekend pass, as he was now near enough to come home.

In the spring of 1942 David wrote a letter which gently broke the news to us that he had volunteered to go abroad (although his entire group had been told that they were too young to go overseas) and that he had been accepted and would 'shortly be going to the land of his birth'. India could not be mentioned, for security reasons. 'The Bloke', as my father and John always called him, was determined to do something to help end the war and bring John home as soon as possible, and also, as he put it, 'to have a go at those little yellow bastards' (the Japanese).

Once more, our mother suffered the agonies of anxiety which all mothers knew at this time – and, indeed, at all times; he was going into the unknown, she was powerless to do anything about it, and only God knew what would become of him. Before going he would be given embarkation leave, but having leave due to him before that, he wanted her to go with him for a holiday in the West of Scotland at the end of May. This was something that they had both always wanted to do.

David made all the arrangements, sending the fare, which was £8 return from Hassocks to Scotland! They went to a beautiful place called Crianlarich, in Perthshire, and he paid for everything. Mummy went to meet him en route, sitting on her suitcase in a train packed with troops.

It was the best and most memorable holiday that she had in her entire life, and she remembered it for ever. Very few sons of 19 years old would take their mother for a holiday and be so thoughtful for her well-being in this day and age … I feel very sad when I think of all the strife that there is between parents and their teenage children these days, and certainly from that aspect the war did us all good, because it made us realise that nobody was immortal and no one could be taken for granted, as they might not be there the next day.

While they were away I stayed with a school friend called Shirley Knight, who lived near the school.

No sooner had my mother enjoyed this welcome, scenic and peaceful break than she began to get worrying letters from South Africa. Rosemary, who had been doing so well at Kingsmead School in Johannesburg, and who seemed to be the favourite with her hosts and benefactors, had suddenly started having epileptic fits. We had always known that she had a weak heart, and the doctors at first thought that the height above sea level in Johannesburg was too much for her. They advised that she should return to England as soon as possible. Convoys were not in quite such danger now, and the war was beginning to turn in our favour, but you still had to wait many months for a ship. So, while David waited to go out to India, Rosemary waited to come home.

In August, David was given 14 days' embarkation leave, which he spent rushing round, seeing all his friends, including those masters who had taught him at Brighton College, his childhood friends at Storrington and more recent friends in Ditchling. He was thrilled to bits about going, as he had been getting increasingly bored at the endless training camps, and was longing for action and adventure. This happy enthusiasm helped to cheer our mother, who naturally dreaded the parting. Happily for him, he was going with two of his best friends, Richard Phillips (no relation) and Cecil Peake, who had been with him throughout his training. He was convinced that the war would be over shortly, and that he would soon be back from India to take us all for many more Scottish holidays.

The day which we had been dreading came all too soon. Our parents went with him in a taxi to see him off, while I, being due to attend a Girl Guide meeting, stood on the pavement outside our house in Hassocks, in full Guide uniform, waving goodbye. When I saw his white, set face under the peaked officer's cap as he sat in the back of the taxi, some strong compulsion made me give him, very solemnly, the Guides' salute. In that moment, I knew, suddenly, that this was goodbye for ever. Perhaps we all knew. Half a century later, the picture of those few minutes is still clearly in my mind, like a photograph which I can take out and look at again and again.

THE SCARLET PIMPERNEL

JOINING THE GUIDES, WHICH WERE RUN BY a cousin of the Dumbrells called Jean Ellis, was the nearest that I could get to 'War Work', which everyone was keen to do – that is, apart from the interminable knitting of khaki scarves, gloves, socks and balaclava helmets which we did both at school and at home. Incidentally, both my parents were fire-watchers, which meant that they took it in turns with other people in our road to parade up and down during air-raids looking for fires. I am not sure how they would have coped if there *had* been a major fire, but luckily for them there wasn't.

Jean Ellis was renowned in the village for running practically everything, and was particularly good at producing plays. One thing I could *not* do was act. Far too self-conscious and shy, I used to infuriate her by not having the confidence to raise my voice above a whisper. We were all involved in a huge pageant which was taking place in Ditchling. I was supposed to be George Washington's black gardener in the scene (*mot juste*) about the cutting-down of the famous cherry tree ("I cannot tell a lie, Father, I did it, etc."). I had to say, "Mornin' Massa. Ah hope you feel salubrious, Massa ..." This was supposed to come out in loud, hearty tones, but all I could produce was a feeble squeak.

The more Miss Ellis, or 'Captain' as we called her at Guide meetings, roared and bellowed at me to SPEAK LOUDER, the more feeble my voice became. Why they ever cast me for the part, I shall never know: I suppose they thought my face might look better black.

One hot day at rehearsal in the village hall, I fainted, and was revived by a Canadian soldier. I retired home to bed for a few days, the doctor was called, and he pronounced me undersized and underdeveloped (my chest was as flat as a board, whereas my contemporaries, to coin a phrase from my friend Pauleen, were 'growing things'). Monkey-gland pills were prescribed – how I wish I had gone on taking them until I reached a decent height! I have always loathed being shorter than everyone else.

My acting career, at least in that particular production, was now over, to my great relief. From that time on, I seldom found favour with Miss Ellis, although I could not help liking her. She passed me over for the rank of Second-in-Command of the Scarlet Pimpernels when I was next in line for promotion. This unfairness so incensed the other Guides that, when a vacancy occurred for a Patrol Leader, they all voted for me. It should be explained here that, for some strange reason, 'Seconds' were appointed by the Guide Captain, but Patrol Leaders were voted for by the Company. So it was that, much to 'Captain's' chagrin, I rose from the ranks to a 'Command' position …!

Despite this, I did not excel at any of the activities, and failed my fire-lighting test five times (I almost felt that Miss Ellis was blowing it out when I wasn't looking) but I passed it at the sixth attempt, in pouring rain! You didn't actually have to rub two sticks together, but no paper was allowed and only two matches could be used. The fire had to be kept going long enough to cook a 'damper' on it. This was flour and water, stuck round a stick and held over the fire. When you removed the stick you could put chocolate or jam or something down the hole in the middle, and you were expected to eat it …

Financially, the Scarlet Pimpernels were always in disgrace. Every week, each Guide was required to bring one penny towards Guide Company funds. My patrol, partly consisting of evacuees from the East End of London, used to hand me a miserable collection of farthings and buttons, because they never had any pocket money. Neither did I. In fact, you could say that the Scarlet Pimpernels were in the Red.

The Cheeky Loaf

Q UITE EARLY IN THE WAR, THE ART mistress had joined up to serve in one of the women's armed forces, and a really extraordinary character arrived to take her place. We could not believe our eyes or ears as she took over and shaped our artistic leanings for the next six years. Short and slightly North-country, with a voice like a man and a brown, leathery face to match it, grey hair strained back in a bun, Miss Lethem's arrival really shook us. Her criticisms were ruthless and merciless. Homework was set for us to do each week and was examined minutely with acid comments in front of the whole class. Some of the drawings would evoke her husky, chain-smoker's laugh.

Once, she told us to draw and paint a loaf of bread. Being wartime, all that my mother had for me to copy was a straight-sided sandwich loaf, a likeness of which I faithfully attempted to reproduce, exactly painting in its rather anaemic shades of pale yellow and faint brown and white. It was a labour of love which took me hours – and my mother (who was always truthful) said it was a good likeness.

When Miss Lethem, who had in mind (apparently) Ye Olde Cottage Loafe type of bread, saw my effort, she exploded with rage, tore my masterpiece in half and threw it into the waste paper basket, shouting "CHEEK!" In vain did I try to explain …

However, she must have been a good teacher, because most of us managed to get through the Royal Drawing Society exams every summer – and not just *pass* – we were not allowed to go on to the next grade until we had achieved Honours. Indeed, it seemed to be the school policy in all things that a mere pass was never good enough.

Miss Lethem was good-hearted despite her fierce exterior, for she got all our mothers together at her house every week and made them bind books for the Red Cross to give to the wounded troops to read in hospital.

Her smoking habit eventually got the better of her and soon after I left school, she died of lung cancer.

MISS MARY: LITERATURE AND MORALS

W HEN THE AUTUMN TERM STARTED, I MOVED up to Miss Mary's form, together with three of my friends: Jill Gordon-Smith, who had always been my rival for top place in the form below, Edwina Wills, daughter of the Rector of Albourne, and Shirley Knight, who was two years younger than we were, but very bright. I was very reluctant to leave the fun of being taught by Miss Knowles, with her originality and humour, but it was time for us to be prepared for School Certificate or 'Oxford Senior'. We took it the last year before they started to call it 'O-Levels'. Miss Mary had always taught the top form, which was very small.

Now came my first introduction to Shakespeare, or 'Shakspeare' – one of the first things we were taught was that the correct way to spell his name was without an 'E' between the 'K' and the 'S'.

A Midsummer Night's Dream, The Tempest, Macbeth, As You Like It, Julius Caesar and *Henry V* were the plays that we studied thoroughly. We read them aloud in class, learned long passages by heart for prep, and Miss Mary explained and discussed them. We were not too enthusiastic; I don't think one ever appreciates Shakespeare until years later; but unless you learn it by heart at school you never remember it later. That is why the modern idea that learning by heart is *bad* is so WRONG: the things that I learned by heart are those which I can remember 50 years later.

Miss Mary was so keen on literature that she had invented a subject called 'Authors'. Exercise books, started by girls of previous generations, were handed down to us, which contained, on the left of each page, the author's name, dates and resumé of his or her life, and on the right a list of the books, poems, essays, etc., written by him or her.

First in the book was Caedmon, A.D. 600-odd, with his poem on the Creation, written in a cowshed. Every week we learned a few pages by heart. These come in useful for crosswords and *Mastermind*, and were quite invaluable when I worked in an antiquarian bookshop. (NEVER think that something you learn at school is pointless; these little bits of knowledge have a habit of coming in useful unexpectedly.) One of my bookshop colleagues was so impressed as to be almost overcome when a customer asked for the works of Alexander Pope, and I, with instant aplomb (and probably Miss Mary's ghost beside me) enquired, "Do you want his essays, or his criticisms?"

Miss Mary concentrated on History, Scripture, Literature and English, which meant Grammar, the rules of which were taught thoroughly in the extreme. "There is no such thing as 'bad grammar'," she used to say; "it is bad English."

The amounts of English and French grammar which we learned during a week were about equal, with Latin coming a close second. How I wish that Miss Mary could be here today, to correct the appalling English of the television presenters, reporters and newsreaders. Television *could* have done the nation such a service by being the perfect vehicle for a constant example of well-spoken English, but instead it has done the exact opposite by letting loose on the air every uneducated, inarticulate Tom, Dick and Harry (or possibly Kevin, Shane and Gary). It seems that inverted snobbery has taken such a hold on this country that anyone who speaks correct English is suspected of being a Tory and therefore BAD. Yet terrific trouble is taken with tape-recorders to make sure that French is pronounced correctly by the modern child ... Why can't the English teach their children how to speak?

Visiting staff taught us Latin, Algebra and Geometry, Advanced Geography, and Science – which was mostly Botany and very little Chemistry – which last I have never needed ... However, being a keen gardener, I have found Botany and Latin to be of enormous use.

Julius Caesar in Latin always puzzled me; I had expected it to be Shakespeare's Julius Caesar translated into Latin, and was frightfully disappointed when it turned out to be boring descriptions of his Gallic and civil wars. I much preferred the *Aeneid*, with Dido gruesomely plunging the dagger into her bosom, or Cleopatra clasping the asp ...

In the world of horticulture they say that gardeners could not communicate without Latin. It was my favourite subject and I found it utterly fascinating to recognise it in the stems of English words, and was able to guess at the meaning of hitherto unencountered long words. It is very sad that children in general no longer learn Latin, as it is the basis of so many other languages and would promote much greater understanding.

We were taught by a Miss Geere, who came once a week from Burgess Hill and managed to teach us despite being profoundly deaf.

Miss Mary was a great philosopher, and her best lessons were what she called 'Moral Lectures' (in her case pronounced 'Boral', because of her affliction). These took place on Friday mornings instead of Scripture, and were little homilies on life and its meaning, the Ten Commandments and the reasons for sticking to various Christian rules, rather on the lines of 'I shall pass this way but once', helping our neighbours, putting others before ourselves and not being vindictive to anyone. She was better than any Vicar, and I preferred her talks to the usual Scripture lessons (to which I seldom listened).

The most amusing part of being in Miss Mary's form was singing the morning hymn. In the corner of the room was a small harmonium at which she seated herself, and then began a performance which invariably sent us into helpless giggles as she peered at the knobs, muttering, "Dow which wud do I press?"

At the same time, she pumped her feet up and down on the pedals, slowly producing a noise like a cow mooing, and eventually, as she got into her stride, one could just about pick up the melody of the hymn. By this time, we, standing in a row behind her, were holding each other up, hysterical with laughter and unable to sing at all until she was half-way through the first verse. The hymn which she chose most frequently (we were still having air-raids) was No. 5, Ancient and Modern, *My Father for Another Night of Quiet Sleep and Rest*.

While I was having all these new academic experiences, my brother David was, tantalisingly, still in this country, at Halifax, waiting for a troop ship. His letters were heavily censored and he could not telephone us. Few people had telephones, and calls were supposed to be confined to those which were utterly essential. Urgent messages could be telephoned to our school, but in any case I don't think he was allowed to make calls, for security reasons. We ourselves did not have a telephone until 1946.

No sooner had he finally set sail (unknown, of course, to us) than Rosemary arrived home. In a way, it was more fun for me to have a companion, although I was in awe of my cousin's rather bossy, know-all manner (at that time), and her loud voice, tinged with a strong South African accent, had a way of putting me in my humble place.

Having been warned about her fits, I was on edge most of the time, wondering when she would have one and what form it would take. I did not have long to wait; in the middle of lunch on the first day, she was talking to me when she suddenly stared ahead and slowly swayed back in her chair, closed her eyes and dribbled a bit at the mouth. I was scared, but not too badly. However, this was only known as '*petit mal*'; later, she fell on the floor for much longer periods, foaming at the mouth (known as '*grand mal*').

It was my policy to leave her there and ignore the whole thing, avoiding embarrassment when she regained consciousness by simply pretending that nothing had happened. However, my mother worked herself into a frenzy, trying to lift her up and drag her upstairs to bed, which was quite the wrong thing to do.

Rosemary had these fits three or four times a day, and after some weeks of this the doctor decided that it was too much for both of us, so she was sent to what was called an 'Epileptic Colony' – rather like a Leper Colony, which you would expect to find in Darkest Africa, but it was near East Grinstead.

She stayed there for two years and emerged virtually cured, i.e., she did not have another fit until she was married and pregnant, when the whole ghastly process started again, causing her to be on drugs permanently, with their devastating side effects.

Perhaps she should never have had children, but she was a marvellous mother and derived great joy from her two pretty daughters.

LETTERS FROM INDIA

D AVID'S LETTERS FROM INDIA BECAME MORE AND more interesting but less and less frequent. At first he had spent some time at a training camp near Poona. He couldn't say much, but we gathered that he was doing some kind of Commando training about which he seemed very thrilled. Some of his letters contained observations on the social and political aspect of India at that time: on 5th December, 1942, he wrote,

> *'Of course, you know old Ghandi is in Poona, living in the Aga Khan's palace. The most serious trouble is what is happening about the future government of India. These blokes CANNOT govern themselves. They can't even look after their own health and houses properly yet. On the other hand I think the British Government could do a lot more after the war towards improving living conditions, building roads, etc.*

How right he was ...... He took a long leave and stayed with our mother's brother, Louis Pinhey, who was in the Indian Political Service and lived up in the hills in Baluchistan with his wife and four children, who welcomed David with great delight.

After this, he volunteered to go to the Middle East with his friend Richard. Unfortunately, Richard was sent to the Middle East, but David was considered more valuable as an instructor in Poona, and could have stayed there with promotion, but so anxious was he to get at the Japanese that he volunteered to go into action in the Burmese jungle.

In a letter written on his 21st birthday (16th June, 1943) while on a secret and dangerous mission about which we could only guess, he wrote, *'It is the sort of warfare where you give a man a tommy gun and a week's rations and say, "meet us at such and such a point when you have killed five Japs"* ... *Never mind, it is all very unusual and therefore interesting and exciting, and when we get home we shall have some real stories to tell.'*

It must have been the ultimate in terrifying creepiness, hacking your way through the undergrowth, not knowing whether hostile eyes were following your every move, or how many guns were pointed at your head. It really required guts to volunteer for that, and David had been a nervous little boy who overcame his fears by forcing himself to do things such as jumping into a pond when he couldn't swim, but didn't want his brother or his friends to think that he was a coward.

My mother worried desperately about both boys. Although I, too, longed for news of them and missed them terribly, I was, at that time, preoccupied with other things; I was in love with the Curate …

It started at Sunday school, where this very amusing young man illustrated the Bible stories with hilarious drawings on a blackboard in Keymer Church (pronounced *Kymer*, not *Keemer*). When teaching us about the Christening service, he drew Godmothers in outrageous hats. I was immediately hooked on his humour. He wasn't very beautiful to look at, but his wife was. Sadly for me (and her) he decided to join ENSA and go away to entertain the troops. He realised that he was more of a comedian than a Churchman. Before leaving, being rather penniless, he sold me his pet rabbit, called Solomon. At the last minute, his wife decided to throw in Solomon's wife, a beautiful Blue Beveran. My knowledge of Scripture being rather hazy, despite Miss Mary Dumbrell's teaching, I shocked my mother by suggesting that Solomon's wife should be called Gomorrah.

Solomon and Gomorrah produced vast quantities of children, revolting to regard when newly born, as they were completely bare and furless. On several occasions their mother ate them because we looked into the nest too soon. Such are the habits of rabbits. Our original idea had been to help the war effort, the meat ration situation and our pockets by selling the young rabbits to the butcher. However, when it came to the point, we simply couldn't bear to do so, and in a very short space of time we found ourselves with 26 pet rabbits. All my free time was spent wandering in the fields and woods, gathering handfuls of dandelion leaves, hogweed, clover and anything else that they liked.

Much later, there were rumours that the Curate had been defrocked after running away with a chorus girl. Whether true or not, we never saw him again …

The Red Ribbon

The raids had eased off a bit, troops were concentrated in our area in large numbers, the roads were full of convoys, and bigger and bigger tanks lumbered through the village as preparations for D-Day were gradually getting under way.

As it now seemed safer, one of my mother's friends from Hove, who had taken her small daughter to Yorkshire, away from the bombs, returned south and came to live in Ditchling. Diana Johnson, although three or four years younger than I was, proved to be a very entertaining and original child, always writing funny stories about extraordinary people, accompanied by hilarious illustrations. I had first met her when she was 10 days old; half-way down our street of Victorian houses in Hove, Tisbury Road, had lived this most amusing friend of my mother's who had just produced her second daughter. I was taken to see the baby have its bath. That baby, Diana, became, and has remained, one of my greatest friends.

I took her tree climbing – my craze of the moment – introduced her to my friends (she came to school at North End – where else?) and enjoyed the experience of being the eldest for a change, and 'mothering' her. Besides tree

climbing, we had a craze for birdwatching, and used to sit up trees, eating unripe nuts and hoping for rare birds to appear. The unripe nuts had an unfortunate effect on Diana, who continually disappeared into the dense bracken to return later with a red face, announcing that she had 'Dire-airer' ...

Unfortunately, Diana, in company I may say with many others, was scared stiff of Miss Knowles and, being a very nervous child, this had disastrous consequences; there was a strict rule that we were supposed to 'excuse ourselves', as it was politely called, *before* lessons, during break or after lessons – but NOT while lessons were in progress. If you were desperate and put up your hand, saying, "Please, Miss Knowles, may I be excused?" you were liable to be thundered at, and/or the request was refused. We therefore sat and wriggled until the end of the lesson. How many young bladders were permanently damaged as a result of this, I do not know.

Miss Knowles's defence was that there were, or had been, pupils who asked to be excused just to get out of a boring lesson (not that Miss Knowles was ever boring). She could have had some justification, because, from what my mother told me about her own schooldays in Eastbourne, *she* had been so bored that she had spent most of her time in the lavatory. The boys used to get away with it sometimes, particularly Trevor Vokins, whose family owned a chain of drapery stores in the South of England.

Anyway, one day, Diana could contain herself no longer and, not daring to ask, quietly wet herself. Well, perhaps not so quietly ... Miss Knowles tied a red ribbon on the chair, to warn other children not to sit on it. This caused agonies of embarrassment for Diana, but great amusement to her family.

Years later, Diana went to stay with her married sister and found a red ribbon tied to her bed ...

Sadly for me, Diana did not stay long in Ditchling, as her mother decided to go back to Hove, and her father returned from abroad; but I was now to have another companion ... More worrying letters arrived from South Africa – it seemed that her benefactors could no longer cope with Pat on her own. She was homesick and, they were shocked to announce, she had 'started having boyfriends'! An *engagement* was even mentioned ... She was 15 years old.

Back she came to school with me, her arrival coinciding with that of the Doodlebugs (flying bombs). She entertained everyone and got away with murder, chatting away to the mistresses in class, which the rest of us would never have dared to do. 'The Powers That Were' insisted that she must take School Certificate before being allowed to leave, although she had obviously had enough of school. In this she was greatly aided by a Doodlebug which crashed down quite near the building in Haywards Heath where she was taking the exam, and all the candidates had to leave their papers unfinished and were given the benefit of the doubt and passed willy-nilly.

We all found Pat terrific fun, and my solitary life at home changed completely. I really enjoyed having someone to ride to school with, history books balanced on the handlebars as we shrieked dates to each other, doing our homework en route and waving to the soldiers in the army lorries.

Girl Guide meetings were enlivened by Pat's presence, as she was constantly at war with a very pretty, disgracefully naughty evacuee called Rosie, whose language, at least to *our* carefully nurtured ears, was appalling.

The crunch came (literally) one evening when Pat and Rosie laid into each other, punching, kicking and ripping each other's clothes, until they fell, to a tinkling, cracking accompaniment, into a row of cold frames belonging to the Guide Captain's father.

The rest of us were standing demurely in a circle, fingers linked, waiting to sing *Taps*, when the two dishevelled, bleeding, ragged combatants appeared round the corner. The whole argument had arisen when Pat had told Rosie's younger sister, a little misery called Elsie, to do something, and Rosie, ever ready for instant rebellion, had said, "Don't you do it, Else."

Since half the Guide Company now consisted of evacuees, our Church parades were somewhat lacking in smartness and precision. The Colour Party marched in front, followed by a trail of out-of-step, scruffy creatures, slopping along in ill-fitting shoes, eating apples and throwing the cores at various members of the populace who had turned out to watch us go by.

An Epitaph of Laughter

THE TELEGRAM CAME ONE MORNING IN EARLY January, 1945. It announced briefly that David was 'missing'. My father tried to be optimistic: after all, we had received the same news about John, and *he* was all right. At least it did not say, 'Missing, believed killed', which was the second-worst category of the three telegrams which were officially sent out to next-of-kin – i.e., 'missing', 'missing believed killed' and 'killed in action'. Maybe David had gone ahead with a bridging party and got cut off from communications … My father went off to the 'North Star'.

I did not go to school for a few days, but stayed at home with my mother. She knew and I knew that this time there was no hope. She told me that, a few days before the telegram came; she had woken up in the morning and found herself staring straight across the room at David's photograph. As she looked, the photograph slowly fell forward on to its face, on the table. She knew what had happened. For my part, I could see no rowing boat or any hopeful sign, as I had when John was missing.

Back at school, Miss Knowles looked at my solemn face and said kindly, "I hear you've lost David." I gave her a watery smile, my lip quivering; "Daddy thinks he might have gone ahead with a bridging party," I quavered, without conviction. Tactfully, she said no more.

Three weeks later, the final telegram came. I was in my darkened bedroom early one morning when I heard my mother coming up the stairs, sobbing, "Oh God, it's all over." I took the telegram from her hand. The War Office regretted that her son, Captain K. D. G. Phillips, R.E., had been killed in action at Budalin, Burma, on the 6th of January 1945. She clung to me, saying, "I always knew I was going to lose him. I'm so glad I've got you, you are so like him." Like him, perhaps, but never in a million years would I have his courage.

We had not heard from David for four months, and this was the first we had heard of his promotion to Captain. When his diary was sent home, with his other belongings, it had not been filled in for the last four months, so we only knew that he was in the thick of the jungle battles.

My father was sleeping soundly. We didn't have the heart to wake him, so we just left the telegram by his bed and went downstairs to force ourselves through the usual domestic chores in a drab, miserable, semi-conscious state. (We didn't have a telephone and I am not sure how other people heard the news, but probably I told the neighbours, and eventually the Vicar arrived with words of comfort. We had a particularly good Vicar at that time; his sermons had me absolutely spellbound, hanging on every word, which is unusual for a 14-year-old. I had been confirmed the year before, wearing Guide uniform because there were insufficient clothing coupons for a white dress. His confirmation classes were brilliant, and caused me to forget my previous crush on the Curate.)

When he finally awoke and read the telegram, my father was heartbroken. 'The Bloke', as he had always called his second son, because of the way he strutted up and down playing soldiers as a small boy, was very dear to him. That night, he came into my room, saying, "We have made the supreme sacrifice and that is how we must look upon it." His grandfather (seventh son of the 7th Earl of Galloway) and his father's brother had both been Vicars and towards the end of his life my father took to reading his Bible frequently, sometimes copying out passages in his perfect handwriting.

Letters poured in from all the staff at Brighton College, the Matron, all David's friends, our many relations, trying in vain to offer comfort to our mother, and every one of them extolling David's great popularity, humour and sense of fun. The letter which best sums it up and serves as his epitaph was from his House Master's daughter, Anne Corbett: '*Everywhere that David was, all was gaiety and laughter, and that is how I shall remember him.*'

In the Fever Hospital

As if my mother hadn't had enough worry and misery to cope with, she now had even more. John had not been heard of for several months, as the Allies were now fighting their way across Europe and the Germans were forcing the prisoners to leave their camps and march eastwards, away from the Allies and towards Russia. Now, whether from the shock of David's death or just my bad luck, I embarked on a lengthy and serious illness. Maybe it was a blessing in disguise, to take my mother's mind off her great tragedy, as she was fully occupied in looking after me.

First, a bad chill developed into such bad earache that I had to have my ear drum pierced under anaesthetic – in our drawing-room, on the sofa. Such a thing would never happen now, but it *was* wartime. Two doctors attended me. Then I developed pneumonia, and after three weeks at home, taking something called 'M & B 693' (a sulfanilamide compound which was a forerunner to antibiotics) which did me no good, I was taken to hospital in Brighton, much against my will.

Every day a team of lady doctors listened to my chest, muttered comments in medical gobbledygook and looked grave. They told me nothing; I became more and more alarmed and my condition worsened. The nights were terrible: I was in a huge public ward, full of old women who moaned and groaned, and I coughed most of the night. I seldom got more than an hour's sleep, and then, just as I had at last dropped off, they woke me for breakfast at 6.30!

Talk about sleep being the best medicine, it is the one thing you never get in hospital. As I was the only child in the ward, everyone used to stare at me and comment on my long, black pigtails.

I hated every moment, and most of all I hated the lady doctor with the Eton crop, who was utterly inhuman so far as I could see, and never gave me a single word of comfort or encouragement.

One morning I was lying in a semi-conscious state with screens round me when I became aware of our Vicar from home, sitting on a chair beside me, praying. I really thought I was getting the Last Rites. "I see from your chart that your temperature is 104º," he said comfortingly.

That evening I showed one of the nurses a red rash under my skin on either side of my tummy. She told me not to fuss. Then a more senior nurse saw it: panic broke out. I was shifted into a side ward. In the middle of the night I was taken in an ambulance to the Bear Road Sanatorium on top of the Downs above Brighton. I had Scarlet Fever!

However ill I was, the forms had to be filled in: "How many brothers and sisters have you got, dear?" Miserably, I replied, "I had two brothers, but one has just been killed."

"How old are they, dear?"

"Twenty-six and 22." She crossed out everything. They had been trying to find out whether I had infected any more children at home.

Every morning when the doctor came, the door of my lonely, stone-floored room was flung open as the nurse shouted, "Scarlet Fever/Pneumonia!" I wasn't a person any more, just a couple of diseases.

Gradually, as the rash receded, my temperature went down and they decided to move me into the general ward with other girls. These ranged from a WAAF aged 17 down to a small Irish Catholic girl aged seven, whose main worry was what she could confess to the Priest who came round every Friday to hear her confession. How could you commit any sins if you were lying ill in bed? "I'll have to make up something," she said. Even at my tender age of 14, it struck me that the Roman Catholic religion must be a strangely hypocritical one.

We were not allowed any visitors and all our letters home had to be baked before leaving the hospital. Every day my father rang up to ask after me, and all they ever said to him was that I was 'quite comfortable'. I wasn't at all comfortable; the food was filthy and I was bored stiff. My one enjoyment of the day was being allowed to have a newspaper and I chose *The Daily Graphic*, which I think later became the *Sketch*. The war appeared to be going well, the Allies were sweeping across Europe and the German army had more or less crumbled.

As we got better we got up to more pranks. We discovered that if you jerked your bed violently you could make it move on its wheels to the centre of the ward, and if the boys in the adjoining ward did the same thing, we could see them and wave. One girl, who was allowed to get up, was constantly being caught sitting on a boy's bed – a terrible crime in Matron's eyes.

After about a month, the WAAF and I were told that we were allowed to get up. All this time, we had not been allowed out of bed, since Scarlet Fever can affect your heart. We found that we *couldn't* walk – we really had to learn again, and one of my legs has been a bit bandy ever since. I had been a keen ballet-dancer, but those days were over.

THE WARRIOR RETURNS

FIVE WEEKS AFTER MY DRAMATIC NOCTURNAL ARRIVAL at the Sanatorium I was sitting on my bed one afternoon when I was told to go out on the balcony in the sunshine (it was mid-April, 1945) because I had *a special visitor*.

Puzzled, I shuffled out and sat on a bench. Along the path below limped a very thin soldier in a kilt. Before he came up the steps, a nurse made him put on a white gown and a mask to ward off germs, and then we advanced towards each other on the balcony and I recognised him as my brother, John. We had not seen each other for six years *and we shook hands*.

Before he went away to the war he had put two oranges inside my jersey and said, "This is what you'll look like when I see you again." Now, he was so polite – just as if he were meeting a strange young lady at a cocktail party. "When and how did you get back?" I asked. He then told me the amazing tale of his adventures from the day when the Americans had bombed his POW camp, causing the Germans to force the prisoners to march 61 miles towards Russia on Good Friday (hence the limp) to the moment on the evening of our father's birthday, the 9th of April, when he had walked into our house in Hassocks, providing the best birthday present of all. (Not forgetting that if David could have walked in alive everything would have been perfect, but sadly that was not possible.)

The Americans had swept round in a pincer movement, rescued the prisoners, killed a pig for them, given them far too much food to eat all at once after four-and-a-half years of near-starvation, and then flown them back to England. Needless to say, they were all sick in the plane.

Amid all the joy of his homecoming, he had been forced to swallow the bitter pill of being told that he would never see his brother again. He now referred to this briefly by saying to me, "Now we've got a score to settle with the Japs." The war in the Far East was, of course, not yet over.

A week later, to my great relief, my prison sentence was also over; I was allowed home, with the proviso that I must spend three months in a wheelchair. I had missed almost two terms of school, and there was no hope of my taking School Certificate that summer, as had been hoped.

Our mother was delighted to have us both at home again, and cheered up wonderfully well, although she would never get over the loss of David. Her only comfort was the thought that he had *wanted* to go and fight, that he had volunteered and was thrilled about the whole adventure.

A never-ending stream of neighbours arrived with every kind of food that they could spare for the starving ex-prisoner and his invalid sister who 'needed building up'. Those who kept hens brought eggs which were rationed to one a week per person normally, and these were a welcome change from the powdered egg on which we had been existing. Kind people brought cakes for which they had sacrificed part of their rations; even parsley-honey and carrot-marmalade were produced by the more adventurous cooks. That was the aspect of the war which was so *good*: it made everyone so very unselfish and thoughtful towards their neighbours. 'Always put yourself last,' we were taught at school.

My long hair was cut off, as it was supposed to be 'sapping my strength'; I felt like Samson. My first appearance with short hair coincided with our first meeting with John's fellow POW, Robert MacGill, to whom I had been writing, in company with other prisoners, at John's request, because he said they did not receive many letters and needed cheering up. Robert and John had whiled away the time, learning Arabic, writing poems and even escaping together, although they never got more than two miles. On one memorable occasion they were recaptured by 30 schoolchildren and two dogs. Their poems were published after the war in a book called *Oflag IX-A*.

Robert's father had died at his desk in Buckingham Palace from a heart attack. His job was something mysterious called the Board of Green Cloth. Therefore, his mother had relied on an old friend of the family, Quintin Hogg (later Lord Hailsham), for helpful advice when planning her son's future. Consequently, when the 1945 elections came along, John and Robert had a lot of fun helping Quintin to canvass for his seat in Oxford.

Towards the end of the summer term I was allowed to abandon my wheelchair and return to school, where I had a lot of catching-up to do. For English literature we were doing *Henry V*, which was extremely lucky, because the film came out that year and I was able to see it twice.

A big decision now had to be made about where we were going to live: we should, of course, have returned to our house in Hove, but none of us felt that we could face it without 'The Bloke'; he had always been the centre of 70, Tisbury Road, singing loudly as he hammered in his little workshop, always making things, and there would be too many memories. Besides, we had all become used to living in the country. We wanted to sell the house and buy one in the country, perhaps in West Sussex, nearer to where I had been born, where my parents and John still had friends.

By sheer coincidence, Miss Knowles, who now lived with her mother near Pulborough, happened to hear of a suitable house (at a suitable price) at Fittleworth, between Pulborough and Petworth. It had been a guesthouse, and had six bedrooms, three reception rooms, a study, a kitchen, two outhouses and a huge hut at the bottom of the garden which had been used as a canteen for troops and had its own kitchen. Our parents were immediately thrilled with it, particularly our father, because it was joined to the village pub at one corner, and he found old friends in the bar. (The price was £1,700 … 56 years later it was on the market for £425,000.)

We were all enchanted by the beauty of the surroundings: the river Rother – a tributary of the Arun, which flowed between Pulborough and Arundel – flowed under a picturesque bridge a few yards down the road – at least, it *had* been picturesque before the Army lorries had knocked it about a bit – but before you reached it there was a smaller bridge, on the right of which was a tall mill, standing high above the constantly-churning wheels which produced creamy froth on the surface of the deep, black pool. The continuous sound of the rushing water of that millstream is one which I can still hear whenever I think of Fittleworth.

In autumn, this magic place became a fantastic picture at which one never tired of gazing. All our visitors used to be dragged enthusiastically down the road to feast their eyes on this wonderful sight of the tall stone building almost covered by fronds of pinkish-red Virginia Creeper hanging gracefully down, hiding the windows and dangling over the stone parapet at the side. It was a scene which started with violent, churning activity and ended in peace in the dark pool lower down.

Many an hour of my teenage years was spent gazing, just gazing, at this breathtaking natural picture and dreaming, but so few of those dreams have ever been realised. Had I known that those were the only days when I would have time to stand and stare, I should have written down all those dreams.

Beyond the river bridge was a third bridge, over the railway. There was a station with trains that connected with all the London trains from Pulborough. The service was far better and faster then than it is 50 years on; it hasn't all been progress, despite modern technology. I shall never forgive Doctor Beeching for doing away with all the enchanting branch lines. Our very special local train was known to some as 'The Fittleworth Flier', but to us it was known as 'The Flying Pig'. As soon as John (who had a soft spot for pigs) heard the engine snort as it pulled, or sometimes pushed, its two carriages while the engine-driver made his tea, he christened it 'The Flying Pig' and thereafter we never called it anything else. In winter the river flooded all over the fields and the little train appeared to be swimming across the water, a magnificent sight, its steam flowing out behind it in a long line.

In the other direction it went to Midhurst, and twice a day to Petersfield, which meant that people could transfer to the main Waterloo-to-Portsmouth line. Incredible to think how much easier it was for country-dwellers to get across country then.

However, no one had yet heard of Doctor Beeching, and we were able to enjoy our delightful 'puffer-train', the gaunt station master who had eight or nine children, his scarlet-faced wife who laid out bodies as a part-time job, and the man in the signal box who never wore a shirt. Those days were full of exploration and amusement.

We had moved in gradually, in relays. My mother and I had bed and breakfast in a cottage near the pub; I have never forgotten the amazing sight of four rashers of bacon and *two* eggs on my plate the first morning – something not possible to imagine during the war – and now it really had ended, for the day we moved in was 'VJ Day' (Victory over Japan).

Two furniture vans, containing all our possessions which we had not seen for six years, left Hove, but only one turned up. The other made off, we knew not where, and was never seen again. It contained all our silver, the boys' cups which they had won for sport, and all my beautifully-illustrated children's books.

That night, Fittleworth celebrated victory with a huge bonfire outside the 'Swan', and everyone joined hands and danced round it to the music of an accordion played by a Hungarian Countess. No one stood on ceremony: the plumber – one of the ugliest men I have ever seen, but also the most good-natured – grabbed my mother and me by the hands and dragged us into the circle. Fittleworth had welcomed us and the war was truly over.

BACK TO SCHOOL IN DITCHLING

WHAT WAS GOING TO HAPPEN ABOUT SCHOOL? Rosemary and I still had two years to go, and we were in the middle of working for School Certificate. The dear old Dumbrells came to the rescue again; they would start taking a few boarders once more, and we could be the first. Our luggage could be sent in advance by train, and we could travel in Miss Knowles's car. Very little would be charged, and our education need not be interrupted by starting again at a new school. Although thrilled with our new abode, we had been sad to leave Ditchling and all our friends, but by going back to school there the transition was made gradual and painless.

In the meantime, John had been accepted by the Sudan Political Service. Having passed two Arabic exams in the POW camp (arranged by the Red Cross) and having returned to Oxford for a few weeks to complete his degree, which had been interrupted by Hitler, he had boldly walked into the Sudan Government office in London and applied for a job. There was some time before he had to go, and they had stipulated that he must learn to ride – essential for a District Commissioner in the Sudan, where in some areas a horse was the only mode of transport, so he arranged to have lessons with a Mrs Rolt in Fittleworth, and very generously paid for Rosemary and me to learn as well.

All too soon, these idyllic holidays came to an end. Miss Knowles arrived in her tiny Morris (green, with a hood, forerunner to the Morris Minor, I believe) and we were driven back to Ditchling. I had had the distinction of being the last boarder to go to North End at the outbreak of war, and now I was, with Rosemary, the first to return after the war had ended.

It was strange being the only boarders. We had to help a lot with washing-up, peeling potatoes, waiting at table and even sweeping the classrooms. The two school maids had disappeared to join the Land Army quite early on in the war, but Cook was still there, a marvellous character with a hare-lip, whose speech took a lot of understanding (and I'm afraid we imitated it) but who was extremely well-read and intellectual. She had a great sense of the ridiculous and could always guarantee a few laughs. Cook, whose name was Jessie Kempton, had started her career as a milliner, but applied for the job of school cook when she saw it advertised, just thinking she would like a change, but never left the school until she was in her nineties, when Miss Knowles took her home and looked after her until she died.

Another member of the domestic staff was Alice, who walked through the fields every morning at some Godforsaken hour, in time to place cans of hot water outside every bedroom door.

Then there was Sarah Turner, who seemed to go on for ever, like the one in the Bible. Tall, thin and a bit lopsided, topped by fuzzy curls, she also walked up from the village, to do the cleaning. It is quite a mystery how she came to be sweeping floors, because in Ditchling Museum I saw the Turner family tree, which showed them as an important land-owning family, and the Turner Room at the museum is named after them.

Cook and Miss Knowles were great friends and teased each other quite a bit, although sometimes Miss Knowles would get on her high horse and put Cook in her place, snatching up her wireless, which spent a lot of time on the kitchen table, and stalking off, saying, "It's *my* wireless." Cook would repeat this mockingly as she watched her go.

Food was still rationed and we each had our own minute (two or three ounces) portion of butter on a separate dish in front of us at mealtimes. This had to last a week, and it was up to us whether we had a thin scraping each time, or spread it thickly and then went without for the rest of the week. This was excellent training for being a housewife later on.

At 8.00 a.m. we had breakfast with the Dumbrells, Mademoiselle and Miss Knowles – having practised the piano since 7.30 a.m. This meal consisted of large bowls of porridge with golden syrup on it (sugar was rationed) followed by bread with butter *or* marmalade, or Cook's delicious quince jam, the like of which I have never tasted again.

In the evening the Dumbrells liked to eat alone with Mademoiselle and Miss Knowles (who *didn't* like it much); so Rosemary and I had supper at 7.00 p.m. in the kitchen with Cook, after helping to put the Dumbrells' supper through the hatch into the dining-room. This was very high up and I could hardly reach. There was a little room called the garden-room where the hatch was. Many old houses had such rooms, originally intended for the Mistress of the house in which to do her flower arranging. When the hatch was closed we couldn't hear the Dumbrells' conversation and they couldn't hear the high jinks that we were getting up to (instigated by Cook) in the kitchen, sometimes having Miss Knowles's wireless on while we danced round the table to the music. Cook's favourite programme was *Those Were the Days*, with Old Time dancing. Such *simple* pleasures satisfied us in those gentle days between the end of the war and the day when we would have to leave school and face the hard world outside.

Our supper invariably consisted of home-made soup followed by bread and dripping, but sometimes cook produced some not-so-delicate morsel of leftover suet pudding for us, and if we were still hungry, as we very often were, she would smuggle parcels of leftovers up the back stairs to our bedrooms a bit later – for, immediately after supper, aged 15 and 16, we went STRAIGHT TO BED!

Imagine the breathless excitement of finding a parcel of cold macaroni-cheese under your pillow at 8.00 p.m. ...! It really was nectar to me, and perhaps that is why I was completely unable to cope with my own teenagers, who wanted the best of everything. It had taken so little to please us, after enduring the deprivation of war.

When we did not have soup, in the summer we had a mug of cold milk, straight from the farm next door. In fact, we drank a lot of milk, and I am sure that is why we were so healthy, despite six years of rationing. At first I loathed milk, and Rosemary used to drink it for me when no one was looking, but in the end I came to like it.

Following a regular routine in which every minute is organised always makes the weeks pass quickly, and in no time we had reached the end of term, with the usual carol singing and Nativity play, the small day-boys playing the part of shepherds.

Our suitcases were full of ghastly home-made presents and we returned to the welcome of roaring fires and Christmas festivities at Fittleworth.

The playwright Gertrude Jennings, well-known for writing plays for schools to perform, lived in Fittleworth, so we always had brilliant pantomimes, written and produced by her. Two local grandmothers made hilarious pantomime dames – in this case, the Ugly Sisters – and I thought this the best pantomime I had ever seen.

There were at least two dances that I remember that Christmas – a formal, black tie affair, run by the Conservatives, and a hilarious fancy-dress dance (run, I think, by the British Legion) at which Joe Williams the plumber won first prize, dressed in black bombazine with a bustle and a bonnet, as an old tinker woman. This costume looked marvellous with his scarlet cheeks. On another occasion I remember him carrying off the first prize, dressed as a sweep; his original creations were always the highlight of the evening at these annual occasions.

As there was also a prize for the best *pair*; my mother, who had quantities of authentic Indian clothes brought back from India, which she had kept for us to dress up in, decided to send me, with a tall cousin, as Mumtaz Mahal and Shah Jehan. We won the prize, but the local paper described us as 'The Taj Mahal'.

On another occasion I won first prize, dressed as my great-grandmother, Lady Gordon (wife of General Gordon's elder brother), wearing her own black dress, complete with bustle and cream-coloured lace fichu, all of which had been carefully preserved and handed down through the family. I carried a painting of her and had my hair done the same way.

With all these excitements, the Christmas holidays went by in a flash; one last canter across Coates Common under the stern supervision of Mrs Rolt, and we were trundling back to Ditchling and some really hard studying, as this was the last term before the dreaded School Certificate.

GEOFFREY AND HIAWATHA

1946 WAS THE LAST YEAR BEFORE SCHOOL Certificate became 'O levels'. At our school they expected you to matriculate on your School Certificate, i.e. to get five 'credits' (which I think would be 'B' grades). If you achieved this, you did not have to take a separate matriculation exam to get into a university. We were only told about Oxford, Cambridge and London – the others did not exist, so far as we knew. I chose Botany, Latin, History, French, Literature and Maths, which were compulsory and included Arithmetic, Algebra and Geometry, which last I loathed and could not do.

During this term we were allowed to go out to tea at weekends with friends in the village, and we made frequent visits to Rosemary Pepler, whose husband owned and ran the *Ditchling Press*. Born Rosemary Meynell, she was related to the famous literary family, including Alice Meynell, the poetess. Her mother, Esther Meynell, wrote books about Sussex. Rosemary had been a pupil at North End, and her greatest friend was a cousin of Miss Knowles called Betty Coode, now Betty Smith. Betty, newly married and pregnant, was helping with the kindergarten until the Dumbrells could find somebody else, and she and her husband were renting Rosemary's attic flat.

We had a lot of fun at these tea parties and it was a relief to get out of the monastic atmosphere for a short time and have a good laugh. I am not saying I didn't enjoy our quaint existence at North End, I loved it, but brief sorties into the outside world did us good, nevertheless.

One amazing thing about North End was that we only had our hair washed at half-term and the day before we went home for the holidays. We existed, unattractively, with lank, greasy locks for six weeks at a time. Teenagers of today, who seem to wash their hair every day, if not twice a day, would be horrified, but the Dumbrells were afraid that we might catch cold – Miss Mary even went so far as to try dry shampoo on us, as if we were dogs or cats.

Once, when I did catch cold, Miss Mary was so worried lest I should have a recurrence of the previous winter's bout of pneumonia that she forced me to wear my hat, coat, scarf, gloves and stockings to walk down the passage every time I wanted to go to the lavatory.

THE STUFFED STOAT

It was the end-of-term hair washing that led me, indirectly, to Geoffrey … We had been taken home for the Easter holidays in Miss Knowles's car, and on our first morning back at Fittleworth I opened the front door in answer to a knock, and was surprised to find myself gazing up into a pair of vaguely familiar sea-blue eyes while a deep voice enquired, "Miss Phillips?" I grinned at the unaccustomed formality and replied, "Yes …?"

"Your brush and comb," he announced, producing my disgracefully shoddy hairbrush and broken comb, "and my sister says you should wash them."

The penny dropped. He was Miss Knowles's much younger brother, whom she had mentioned as being away in the Navy.

We invited him in and gave him coffee. He was very extrovert and soon became deep in conversation with my father. He then asked if there was any decent fishing in the river, as this was one of his favourite hobbies (the other turned out to be kite-flying, which caused me great amusement; he seemed too old). Rosemary and I offered to walk down and show him the river and the millstream.

We knew that you had to get fishing permits from Petworth House, as the land was all part of the Leconfield Estate. These cost 7/- each (35p), one blue and one white, for above the bridge and below. Geoffrey explained to us about the 'close' season when fishing was not allowed, in order to give the fish a chance to breed. The new season would start on the 15th of June. Geoffrey said he would try to get his holiday then, and promised to teach us to fish.

Fishing and Geoffrey were to become my all-absorbing hobbies, once the dreaded 'School Cert.' was over. This educational milestone gathered speed and arrived all too soon.

As our school was so small, and only five of us were taking the exam, we had to travel daily to Haywards Heath, to a school called Trevelyan, to join their large number of candidates in a huge hall. Once again, Miss Knowles's green Morris came into service: somehow she squeezed five fat teenagers into it, plus herself, and we managed this mode of transport for two weeks.

French Oral was an embarrassing ordeal, for you were expected to chat away about anything and everything to a complete stranger – and I was a shy enough conversationalist in English, never mind French. However, by some miracle this 10-minute, red-faced mumble resulted in a distinction.

The History exam was the one I remember best, probably because of its disastrous and mysterious results … Only Shirley Knight and I had chosen this subject, and we were delighted to find that all 14 questions, of which we were only required to answer five, were on matters which we had covered over and over again with Miss Mary. In the 'mocks' we had both achieved

'A' grades. We finished before time and read through all our replies carefully. You were allowed to leave the room half an hour before time, but no earlier. We signalled to each other that we had finished, and left. Outside, we both happily agreed that it had been 'a marvellous paper'.

When the results came out we had both failed. From that day to this we have never been able to understand it, and can only think that there was some muddle on the part of the examiners. Did we leave too early? Surely the invigilator would have prevented us? We both felt confident that we had done a good job. The only thing we did know was that the Powers That Were in Oxford had been known to complain that they did not like Miss Mary's method of teaching History (at which she was extremely competent). I had thought that perhaps I had made some dreadful howler, such as mixing Robert Peel with Robert Walpole ... but we *both* failed. How I wished that I had spent that last half-hour copying out my answers, so that I could have taken them back to show to Miss Mary, in which case she could have put my mind at rest – or pointed out the howler ... To fail, or even just to get a pass, was 'not done at North End'. I often wish that Miss Mary had written and queried the results, but such a course of action was probably unacceptable, who knows? That unfortunate result remains one of the unsolved mysteries of my life.

However, that nasty episode did not occur until August, and for the rest of that last summer term our time was occupied with preparations for acting *Hiawatha* in the school garden, which lent itself admirably, with its dark bushes from which Red Indians could emerge.

We collected and dyed hens' feathers and made all our Red Indian clothes from hessian sacking. Not being a good actress, I had two small parts, one as Minnehaha's father and the other as Mondarmin, the Spirit of the Cornfield. Clothed in yellow and green, I had to have a wrestling match with Hiawatha (otherwise Jill Gordon-Smith). So realistic was our battle that Miss Mary cried out, "Don't hurt her!" This was slightly embarrassing, as we were both meant to be 'hes'. Her anxiety stemmed from the fact that Jill was nearly twice my height.

My brother John made some fairly rude comments about this theatrical production, and also about the end-of-year school photograph, which he said looked like the survivors of an air-raid.

Rosemary was delighted to leave school. I was not; I loved the security and stability of the quiet Victorian atmosphere. However, there was some talk of my going back for a bit, so I was not too downhearted as we set off for Fittleworth, the summer holidays and endless fishing escapades ...

FISHING LESSONS

Geoffrey did not forget his promise. He arrived on his autocycle (a bicycle with a small motor), complete with a picnic lunch which was the envy of us all. His mother was a marvellous cook, and as rationing was still in force she had not wanted him to impose on our limited reserves of food.

The wireless had given a forecast of everything that makes for a perfect fishing day. We began to prepare our fishing tackle: worms seemed scarce in the garden; they are uncommonly intelligent creatures who seem to know instinctively when they are wanted and immediately clear off. However, after some time, a few insignificant, writhing pink invertebrates were produced and placed in a tin, where they all elected to commit suicide, or at any rate to die in some way or other during the half-hour in which we frantically sought for hooks, finally being obliged to seek a kindly fisherman at the 'Swan', who grudgingly allowed us one hook.

Having disentangled ourselves from each other's lines, we set out at last for the river accompanied by our unfortunate guide. We decided to try our luck above the Mill in order to steal a march on those people fishing below the bridge, and catch the fish before they got down to them.

To get to the river it was necessary to leap one or two streams, climb under barbed wire and walk among thistles, all of which may be all right when one is going for a stroll, but with a fishing rod and in a high wind (which had sprung up) this is not so easy. Hooks become devilishly elusive, they dance in the wind, catch in one's clothes and in surrounding vegetation and finally vanish, leaving a practically invisible length of gut to blow about, fiendishly getting itself knotted, however hard one tries to catch it.

All this happened to us before we finally reached a likely stretch of water, baited our hooks (with a mixture of dead worms and a bread paste concocted from the remains of Geoffrey's sandwiches) and, spreading out with some distance between us, cast our lines.

My first attempt at casting lodged the hook in a tree, way up behind my head. Feeling utterly foolish, I had to get Geoffrey (who was beginning to look rather cross, reminiscent of his sister on a bad day in the classroom) to rescue me, or rather my line. At the next attempt I managed to get the float into the water and start to hope – for Hope springs eternal in the fisherman's breast. Alas! The wind blew so strongly that it was impossible to tell if the fish were biting. After a few minutes we decided to move to a more sheltered spot and, led by our instructor, retraced our steps. The elements seemed to have a grudge against fishing, for a sudden gust of wind caused my reel to revolve at terrific speed, all the time unwinding, until festoons of line spread round the thistles. When some minutes had elapsed in rewinding this, I hastily caught up with the others and we crossed the road and prepared to try once more in a sheltered pool beneath the bridge.

Suddenly, for one of us at least, the great moment had come: Rosemary had caught a fish. We will not quibble over the size or species of fish, suffice it to say that she *caught* one, which meant everything. It was now five o'clock, so we went home to tea and gave the 'catch' to the cat.

After tea we decided to risk the wild, neglected gardens of the Mill House, which had been occupied by soldiers during the war, but which had just been purchased but not moved into, by some very rich and (we later discovered) charming people. Finding a large pool surrounded by a high wall, we settled down for some time. The mill-pool was beautiful; as you stared into the black, unfathomable depths you could let the imagination rise to great heights, live lives, build towering castles, hearing only the unceasing torrent of water flowing over the wall and down into the pool. What fascination water holds … "There's nothing on your line, your bait has been taken." Geoffrey woke me from my dreams, and, blushing with embarrassment, I re-baited. Rosemary had caught another fish, and so had he …

On the way home we went and balanced ourselves precariously on the bridge, nearly being swept off by the traffic which passed over it. Just as a charabanc full of trippers paused on the bridge, Geoffrey hooked another fish, causing great excitement among the occupants, who craned their necks out of the windows.

Although loath to leave the quiet river and the lure of rod and line, we at last turned for home. Despite having caught nothing at all, it was, curiously, the end of a perfect day, and the prelude to many more fishing expeditions during those rather damp summer-holiday weeks of 1946. Whenever Geoffrey could come down to stay with his mother and chug over to us on his autocycle, he did.

The real excitement started when we were introduced to pike-fishing. One afternoon, having been forced to beat a hasty retreat from the Mill, owing to a sighting of the new owners, we had just settled in a new spot, downstream, when a voice shouted, "Ho there, any bites?" We looked up, to see a short, middle-aged figure in a grey trilby hat and fawn mackintosh, with a red face divided across the middle by a luxuriant white moustache. We shook our heads in answer to his question – Geoffrey had taught us never to make a noise and always to whisper, for fear of scaring the fish away.

"Nil desperando!" shouted the little man, proud of his inaccurate knowledge of Latin and waving an enormous pike in the air, "Look wot I got."

We were so impressed that we abandoned our position and walked along to where he had been sitting, on a little camp stool, surrounded by an assortment of angler's aids. He was obviously far more organised than we were.

"West's my name, but my friends call me 'Westy'," he announced. We looked at each other: pike-fishing might be exciting; only the other week there had been a picture in the local paper of a man on our very same bridge, holding up a pike nearly as long as himself (claimed to weigh 40 pounds). Geoffrey was soon deep in conversation, unashamedly picking Mr West's brains on the niceties of pike-fishing, while I, in my usual fashion, stood silently by.

Unfortunately, Geoffrey had to return to London, but he instructed me to find out all I could from Mr West, who had another week's holiday, staying at the 'Swan', and promised that he would be back to start catching pike the following weekend …

Timidly, I asked Mr West if he would mind my watching him one afternoon, so that I could learn from 'an expert'. He puffed up visibly with new importance, and said that I was welcome, he was sure.

The next afternoon I accompanied him on safari with all his equipment, including a large suitcase containing hundreds of 'gentles', or maggots, which he informed me had been specially sent down from Yorkshire and were one week old.

"My friend Mr Langer will be along soon," he announced. "He's a real expert, won the largest frying-pan, 'e did." I concluded, rightly, that this was some sort of accolade in fishing circles, akin to the Nobel Prize. "I'm only an amateur; really, but 'e won't tell you nuffink wrong."

He produced a green leather cushion for me to sit on. The sun came out and added to the beauty of the surroundings. A kingfisher dipped low over the water, and bubbles betrayed the presence of a water rat close to the bank.

"Ho, Westy, so this is 'ow you go fishing, yer lady friend with yer, eh?" Mr Langer had arrived.

Westy replied proudly, "I've got the Major's daughter 'ere, takin' a bit o' learnin'." The Major's daughter felt extremely bashful.

Then Mr Langer ticked off poor Westy for having blind-cord on his pike-rod and a few other things of which his expert mind disapproved. My instructor began to blush slightly at being shown up in front of his pupil. After a short tiff, they became friends again. Soon I landed a fair-sized gudgeon, which they informed me was really the best bait for pike-fishing, *as gudgeons have more life in them* (not for long, I thought).

As I have already said, I had been taught to be absolutely silent while fishing, but these two carried on chatting at the tops of their voices, occasionally bursting into song. Whenever there *did* happen to be a silence, Mr West would say to me, "Wot I like about this place is that it's so quiet and peaceful."

No pike were caught that afternoon, but I made careful note of the details of their pike – or, as they called it, *Jack* – tackle: (a) They tested the depth with a plummet; (b) there were eight weights on the line; and (c) the handle of the landing net was longer than one of the fishing rods. I was told that you must play a pike for about a quarter of an hour before you can get it out of the water, and you need a great length of line. The wire between the float and the hook is called the traces.

Because it was supper time, I tore myself away from Izaak Walton's devotees and trudged homewards, followed by shouted promises of a book on fishing, another lesson some time, and final bellows of "Nil Desperando!"

Foolishly, without waiting for Saturday, I went on a secret expedition to try and catch a pike on my own, to impress Geoffrey.

I flung in the float and awaited events. Suddenly, I began to feel scared stiff; all the gruesome stories that I had heard, of pike leaping out and biting people's hands, or dragging them in, began to lurk in my mind. There was no one around; nothing happened for ages except a short skirmish with an eel. Total disaster struck when I got the line caught up, was unable to move it, it snapped, and the tackle, float and all, disappeared from view.

Saturday came. My abortive solo attempt meant that I had *nothing* with which to impress Geoffrey (apart from a new set of tackle, which I had been forced to buy), so I stood meekly in the mud while he had beginner's luck and HOOKED A PIKE!

It happened so quickly that I stood transfixed, watching in horror while Geoffrey danced about, at first with glee, 'playing' the pike, and then with rage, shouting, "Damn and blast and bloody hell!" as it bit through the line and swam off. It was the first time I had heard anyone say 'bloody hell', so sheltered were our lives at Miss Dumbrell's ... My father used to say "For the love of Mike", but I never knew who Mike was. We never did catch a pike.

Now it was time for me to return to Ditchling, while Rosemary stayed at home.

Those summer holidays must have been the happiest of my teenage life.

How very different they were from my daughter's life at 16, nothing but boyfriends, discos, pop music, ugly clothes and hairstyles and everything that is utterly alien to me; how I wish that *she* could have experienced the peace and serenity of the river bank ... "But you were *killing fish*," I hear her protest; somehow, we didn't think of it like that, there was so much patience required, so much anticipation and uncertainty and skill, and the fish had far more chance of getting away than we had of catching them; and remember, food was still rationed and we ate everything we caught, the somewhat muddy taste of river-fish being alleviated by soaking in vinegar before cooking ...

My Teaching Career

IT HAD BEEN DECIDED THAT I SHOULD return to school as a pupil-teacher, learning to teach under the fierce and beady eye of Miss Knowles, and retaking Maths in order to get a credit instead of a pass to complete my matriculation and prepare for possible entry to university.

Miss Knowles was now my 'colleague', and although I still slightly feared and greatly revered her, she treated me more or less as an equal, and we laughed a lot. I hadn't been ready to leave the secure, protective atmosphere of North End, and I had the added bonus of being at first-hand to hear the occasional snippet of news about Geoffrey …

I was given a class of nine children, aged from seven to nine years, and I had to teach them all subjects – even mental arithmetic, which was absolute torture to me as I raced to get the right answer before they beat me to it.

The frightening part was that I had to share a large schoolroom with Miss Knowles, who had an uncanny ability to hear every word I was saying, however absorbed she appeared to be in her own teaching, and if I said something that wasn't quite right she would pounce immediately and correct me, which was unnerving, to say the least, as I was extremely self-conscious about holding forth to a class at the age of 16½. However, she couldn't risk my misinforming the children, and it was the best way to force me to be accurate.

The children in my class were particularly nice, attentive and interested. This was a very pleasant age to teach. They seemed sympathetic to the fact that this was my first attempt at teaching, and I don't remember ever having any trouble with rudeness or cheek. There were boys at the pre-prep stage as well as girls.

On Wednesday afternoons I taught fretwork to the very small boys from four years old upwards. We stuck pictures from magazines and flower-catalogues on plywood and, using a treadle machine, cut out jigsaw puzzles. By some miracle the boys all kept their fingers intact.

Sometimes in the evenings I coached two older girls in Latin. Another girl was backward at reading, so I used to be sent down to her house after school, to help her with extra reading. I am sure the Dumbrells never charged for this; that was the caring sort of school they ran, only interested in the pupils' ultimate success. Nowadays this would be done by a 'Remedial' expert with several qualifications; in those days we used our common sense. Few of the staff had degrees, they were just dedicated. Miss Knowles was born to teach – brilliantly. Miss Mary had a diploma for teaching English, and Miss Edith, who taught the piano only, had studied music in Germany.

Now that the war was over, Mademoiselle returned to France to find her relations who had survived the German occupation and, as it took ages for a replacement from France to get a work permit, the job of teaching French to the *whole school* was entrusted to me. I was petrified, but somehow I muddled through, using Mademoiselle's methods, from which I had benefited for seven years, until a not-too-natural redhead arrived from Paris, rather scandalising the Dumbrells with her ultra-modern outlook. She taught me the words of various hit songs of the moment, including *J'attendrai*.

By now there were five boarders, including a Greek girl called Kristine Cronopulo, whose parents were in India. Her father worked for Ralli Brothers. She was followed later by her cousin, Sally Woods. Kristine and I shared a bedroom. She was 13, but, as usual, taller than me, and I was most impressed by her fantastic wardrobe – her mother had supplied her with numerous sets of skirts, blouses and cardigans, all in matching or toning colour schemes. Everything about her was neat and tidy, from her sleek, tightly-plaited hair to her white socks and shiny shoes. She spoke good English with the occasional funny mistake, although Greek had been her first language until she was seven years old.

At night, after our light had been turned out (in this respect I was still treated like a pupil) she used to teach me Greek songs; no one could hear us; Miss Knowles was closeted in her room with her beloved wireless. I can still remember one of those Greek songs, which, loosely translated, meant 'I'll dress you in red and take you away'. Kristine was the sort of girl who asked to be teased and was the butt for many of Miss Knowles's jokes, but she was very good-natured and never took offence; her brown eyes just twinkled in her plump face. She spent her holidays in Liverpool with her English grandmother.

Another of my tasks was to go to the house of a girl who had broken her leg falling off her pony, and give her lessons so that she would not get behind the other children. At the end of the term, her mother gave me my first ever pair of silk stockings, but I was not particularly thrilled at the time, being a very late developer and not yet really interested in clothes, although, considering that they were rationed, I should have been more impressed.

Although I was studying Maths – and German rather half-heartedly with Miss Mary – and getting board and lodging, my parents did not have to pay any fees, but the Dumbrells paid me £5 a term, which, to me, was a fortune.

Definition of a Lady

NOT MANY PEOPLE WRITING ABOUT THEIR SCHOOLDAYS would say that most of the spare-time entertainment had been provided by the school cook, but indeed, most of the fun *was* due to Cook's participation in our lives … She was always clowning, sometimes deliberately 'winding up' Miss Knowles. At weekends I helped her prepare the vegetables and wash up. If Miss Knowles was in a bad mood, Cook acted as a shield to us, dancing round the kitchen table until Miss Knowles was forced to smile at her antics and the thunderclouds were averted.

No one should have let Cook's speech impediment mislead them into underrating her intelligence; she was a remarkably well-read woman, deeply interested in phrenology, philosophy and religion, but it was her sense of fun that delighted the children, especially at Christmas, when she made toys and dressed dolls for them.

During my second term of teaching we experienced and endured the Big Freeze of 1947, which lasted for seven weeks, from February to April. At first the snow was fun: we had cross-country runs through the fields instead of games, struggling through deep snow. Every day we jogged in crocodile up the main road to the almshouses and back. Then everything froze solid; the plumbing arrangements were not such fun – the lavatories were blocked and we had to pour cans of water down them.

Miss Knowles spent much of her time lighting paraffin stoves and trying to thaw out the cloakrooms. One day, after hanging upside-down with her head half-way down the lavatory-pan, she made the classic announcement that "A lady is someone who doesn't mind what she does". I never forgot it.

Apart from coping with the plumbing, Miss Knowles took endless trouble over the fires to keep us warm (or less cold, for it was unbelievable by today's standards). We helped her to collect and break up sticks for lighting the cosy-stoves (which were not really cosy at all when the doors were shut). At one end of each schoolroom stood a cosy-stove, usually with its doors shut for safety, and that was *all*.

Sometimes, when the Dumbrells were not around, Miss Knowles would open the doors and let the children take it in turns to have a warm-up, standing close to the stove with small hands outstretched towards the flames – but mostly one sat and shivered. My feet were always frozen, and I had such terrible chilblains that the doctor came once a week to give me injections of calcium which appeared to make me far worse, as I ended up with chilblains all over my knees, hands and feet. The bedrooms were like refrigerators, completely unheated, and we did not even have eiderdowns – just two paper-thin blankets.

I devised a way of keeping warm in bed by sleeping with my legs in the sleeves of my dressing-gown and the rest of it draped round my middle. (I must have been 50 years ahead of the fashion world, for I have recently noticed a similar garment being advertised in a catalogue.) Unfortunately, Miss Mary, who used to tramp heavily round the bedrooms making a nightly inspection before she went to bed, discovered this – how, I am not sure, unless my blankets had fallen off, and immediately forbade me to do it ever again, "because it was unhygienic". How I longed for the hot-water bottles of home, where my mother, missing India, made us ultra-warm, but these would have been considered utterly decadent in the spartan world of North End House.

After seven weeks of Arctic conditions and grey skies, we awoke one morning to bright sunlight. A rapid thaw began, and cascades of snow slithered off the laurel bushes and formed pools of water on the lawns. Lavatory plugs were pulled with great delight and water flowed exuberantly from liberated taps.

Miss Mary, ever original, offered a prize of one shilling for the best poem on 'The Return of the Sun'. While Tennyson, Keats and Co. gyrated in their graves, I penned these few blush-making lines and won the shilling,
Whence comes this glow of warmth and light?

> *Strange visitor whose beams so bright*
> *Do penetrate the clouds,*
> *You come to undress bushes green,*
> *To show us things we have not seen,*
> *Whilst clothed in snowy shrouds.*

There might have been more in the middle to warrant Miss Mary's parting with 12 old pennies, but, as far as I can remember, it ended:

> *We're ever on the wireless told,*
> *"For many days expect the cold,*
> *Of ice and snow there'll be much more",*
> *But now, it is The Thaw!*

Miss Mary insisted on reading it aloud to the assembled company at lunchtime, but nobody listened, and the French table kept on chatting – it was ever thus in my moments of triumph …

With my Maths credit safely under my belt (or at least on file somewhere in someone's Academic Archives) and the end of my second term of teaching in sight, there was talk of my possible future in teaching. Miss Mary dragged me into the pantry: this was serious stuff; it was her favourite place for giving people lectures. Her victims were really trapped here, in this tiny room between the hall and the schoolrooms. It was an old-fashioned butler's pantry, with panes of coloured glass in the door, a small sink where the glasses and silver were washed, and a telephone like a daffodil, fixed quite high up on one wall, so that you had to stand on tiptoe to speak into it. The earpiece came away and you held it to your ear.

One usually got summoned to the pantry to receive a wigging, but on this occasion Miss Mary looked embarrassed: "You are a girl who should pass exams and take them seriously," she began, turning slightly pink; "Miss Knowles is very pleased with you and we think you have a gift for teaching, but nowadays you need to have qualifications, so we think your local Vicar should be asked if he would coach you for Oxford; then you should take a teacher's training course, after which we should be delighted to have you back here."

I thought about this a great deal during the rest of that term: did I really want to teach? Wasn't it rather a strain being dignified and on my best behaviour all the time, at not quite 17? Wouldn't I prefer to see something of the world? Had I known that Geoffrey would have liked to teach and take over the school with his sister when the Dumbrells got too old, I might have been swayed …

However, the choice was taken out of my hands by a desperate call from my mother to the Dumbrells, saying that my father was very ill with angina, and she needed me at home to help. Only a few days were left until the end of term, so I did not have much time to think, until I sat sadly in Miss Knowles's green Morris, being driven home, not just for the holidays, but for ever.

Epilogue

I T WOULD BE UTTERLY IMPOSSIBLE FOR ANY modern school-leaver to understand, but I sobbed into my pillow for several nights at the thought that I had left school. The day I had arrived at Dumbrells was the beginning of the happiest years of my life, and the magic spell of the school has never left me. I learned things which I would never have learned anywhere else, all of which have come in useful in later years.

Now, a fear of the unknown future and a sad feeling of finality at the end of this first phase of my life overwhelmed me. No more would I be cocooned in the safety of the Dumbrells' unchanging world.

The best-laid plans of Mice and Miss Mary Dumbrell went terribly agley. Owing to the insatiable activity of our cats, the mice in our area never even got a chance to make plans; the Rector said he hadn't the faintest idea how to coach anyone for Oxford, and my father died three months after I had left school.

Rosemary, on whom I had rather selfishly relied to stay at home, met someone who encouraged her to go and train as an Occupational Therapist, despite her epilepsy, so it was she who ended up at a college on the outskirts of Oxford, while I stayed at home. John was working in the Sudan, Pat was helping in a small boarding-school, and I just felt that my mother could not be left on her own, anyhow not immediately, so I drifted in and out of various local jobs, mainly agricultural or horticultural, which certainly gave me a taste for the outdoor life.

However, five years later, after spending six months in the Sudan (where I was employed looking after John and his wife's children), I realised that I had wasted my excellent education, and finally made the break to London, becoming a secretary like most of my friends, graduating to a job in Fleet Street, where I stayed for nearly five years – but I always went home at weekends. That is why I never returned to teach at North End.

Many people thought, mistakenly, that the Dumbrells were large landowners and therefore 'rich'. They did not, in fact, own all the property, but had a mortgage which was only paid off just before Miss Edith's death at the age of 86. Miss Mary lived on until she was 95, being kept alive on jars of baby food. In the holidays when Miss Knowles went home, she stayed in the cottage where we had lived during the Battle of Britain, being cared for by the person who had inherited it.

Shortly before her death, Miss Mary ordered Helen Knowles and Jean Ellis (her cousin, the Guide Captain) to burn all the photographs and records of the school while she sat in a chair in the garden and watched them. Why she forced them to do this is hard to understand, since we all wanted to preserve the memory of the school, and almost every Old Girl itched to write its history, as I have so inadequately tried to do, but although they live on in my mind, the magic and quaintness of the atmosphere have been impossible to recapture and portray to the new, televisionised generation ...

Miss Mary had given me a parting present of a poem, which she instructed me to copy out and carry with me always, and I did. It was Robert Browning's *Epilogue*. The first two verses were rather incomprehensible at the time (and I am still not sure about their context) but I memorised the last two, and they came to mind and sustained me through all the hard times. In moments of unrequited love (of which there were many) and during my chequered career as gardener, nanny, secretary, editorial assistant, ship's purser, housewife and mother, through redundancy and poverty, Miss Mary's parting gift and the memory of her 'moral lectures' kept me going ...

We fall to rise, are baffled to fight better, sleep to wake.

On my regrettably rare visits to the school in later years, the stuffed stoat which had greeted me in the hall on my first day was still there to greet me once more. In its glass case on the wall it remained, embodying the stability of the Dumbrells and their school. When, in 1982, just before her eightieth birthday, Miss Knowles decided to retire, and the school, which she had continued to run as a highly successful day prep-school, closed down for ever since there was no one to take it on, a contemporary pupil asked if she could have the stuffed stoat as a memento. She obviously felt about it as I did: nothing had changed.

Miss Mary's Parting Present

Epilogue

by

Robert Browning

At the midnight in the silence of the sleep time,

When you set your fancies free,
Will they pass to where – by death fools think imprisoned –
Low he lies who once so loved you, whom you loved so, Pity me?
Oh to love so, be so loved, yet so mistaken –
     What had I on earth to do
With the slothful, with the mawkish, the unmanly?
Like the aimless, helpless, hopeless, did I drivel –
     Being – who?
One who never turned his back but marched breast forward
Never doubted clouds would break.
Never dreamed, though right were worsted, wrong would triumph,
Held, we fall to rise, are baffled to fight better,
Sleep to wake.
No, at noonday in the bustle of man's work-time
Greet the unseen with a cheer – Bid him forward,
     breast and back as either should be,
"Strive and thrive" Cry speed, – fight on, fare ever
There as here!

PART 3:

AFTER THE WAR

What are You Doing Now?

THE END OF WORLD WAR II COINCIDED with lumpy, uncomfortable adolescence. My mother and her contemporaries had been presented at Court when they were our age, but now they did not have the means to present us, and what would be the point, since nearly all the eligible young men had been slaughtered, and those returning from the war were too mature for us? A cousin offered to present me together with her daughter, but I declined, saying (but not to *her*) that if my own mother couldn't afford it, I didn't want to be presented as somebody's poor relation à la Jane Austen … Privately, I reflected that in my current bulgy, bespectacled state, no one would *want* me as a present – certainly not Their Majesties …

We still paid many visits to Hove at this time, and when, in our School Certificate English exam, we had been asked to write an essay on 'The Change-over from War to Peace', I had chosen to write about Brighton Pier. The examiners appeared to have understood my thoughts and kindly gave me a distinction. I am not referring to the now partly-submerged West Pier, but the Palace Pier, which had been out of bounds and surrounded by barbed wire throughout the war, but was now reopened, and we were permitted once more to throw rings over prizes and see What The Butler Saw … Somehow, this seemed symbolic of the difference between the restrictions of war and the freedom of peace.

As I have said, none of us could bear to return to our house in Tisbury Road, since my brother David, who had always been the life and soul of it, had been killed in Burma. Our new life in Fittleworth had just begun.

Old friends were turning up all the time to see our new house, as well as our many cousins as they gradually became demobbed from the forces. Rationing was still in force, but unexpected visitors were fed at the pub next door, which did a nice line in bacon and eggs for three shillings and sixpence, and we were allowed to take a tray of cider-filled tankards to drink at home. Half a pint of draft cider cost seven old pennies then …

At the many post-war cocktail parties to which we were dragged at that time, an irritating question was always asked: "What are you *doing* now?" It gave rise to feelings of inadequacy and inferiority if you could not reply:

(a) that you were studying for a Ph.D. in applied something-or-other; or (b) that you were about to marry a handsome man with titled parents who lived in a castle, or at least a Stately Home. Actually, (a) wouldn't have gone down terribly well, as it was constantly dinned into us that "blue-stockings were not attractive to men". Doing a secretarial course was *just* all right, and fashionable. People were beginning to realise that daughters as well as sons had to earn money. The 'in' thing was to share a flat in London with other girls and work as a secretary. I did not feel ready for this.

"What is your Ultimate Aim?" boomed the father of one of my friends, looking down at me from 18 inches above. His daughter was ex-Roedean and currently at a finishing school in Switzerland. Forgetting to mention the Ph.D. in brain surgery, I squeaked, "To find a husband and have six children, all boys." Luckily, he roared with laughter and barked, "Splendid!"

People who know from the age of five that when they grow up they are going to be an engine-driver, a nurse, or just another brain surgeon are greatly to be envied. When I left school I hadn't the faintest idea what I wanted to do and couldn't really envisage anything but a procession towards the altar followed by several child-bridesmaids and pages. A dazzling bridegroom, preferably with blue eyes and dark, curly hair, would be waiting eagerly to plight his troth with me, and never a cross word would pass between us. I would have six children …

"Your only hope," said my brother John, "is to go and read to somebody at St Dunstan's and he might be persuaded into thinking that you have a nice *voice*, but you'd do better as a lady novelist, as you have all the necessary attributes, including ability, spectacles and a fat behind."

At school they had advised me to teach – well, they would; it was the only career they knew about. "Get the Vicar to coach you for Oxford" they had said. The Vicar (or Rector in our case), on being approached, said he hadn't the faintest idea how to coach anyone for Oxford, and then roped me in to teach English to a foreign boy who was staying with him (nationality not now recalled).

In any case, I could not leave home at present, because my father was very ill with angina and my mother needed all the help she could get.

"He may last another 10 years, or he may go tomorrow," was our rather vague doctor's verdict. (He was inclined to stop his car at the side of the road to listen to a concert on the radio, and then go home again, forgetting that he had been on his way to visit a patient.)

The little brown pills which my father placed under his tongue at the onset of pain were having less and less effect on him, and I was frequently dispatched round the corner to the 'Swan' to fetch nips of brandy, which seemed to have more instantaneous results. In between the bad bouts he would be better, and we managed to enjoy our rural life. My mother's father had originated from Devon farming stock, and she had inherited his love of cows. As I watched them clatter past under my bedroom window, herded by a man called Arthur Whittington, I loved them too.

On good days my father sat on a chair in the middle of the vegetable garden, which was his pride and joy, and told me what to do and how to do it. From him, and from Suttons' book, *The Culture of Vegetables and Flowers*, which he referred to as his Bible, I learned a great deal, and was thus imbued with his passion for gardening.

My first job came unexpectedly and was a task which no one in their wildest imaginings would have thought of: for the princely sum of three shillings (l5p) a *week*, I had to cure the three-year-old farmer's son of knock-knees! His mother came across from the farm opposite and said that the people at the hospital in Chichester had given her a list of exercises which her son must do every day, to straighten his legs. He refused to do them for *her*, but she thought he would do them for me, because she had noticed that I was "good with children".

They hardly ever remembered to give me the three shillings, and I did not like to remind them, for I had noticed that they sometimes raided the little boy's piggybank for it.

However, I got invited to help with the haymaking – I'll never forget the delicious taste of home-made cider and lemonade, which the farmer's wife brought out to the fields in a jug for our elevenses. I trotted across to the farm and cajoled the reluctant small boy into doing his exercises every day for many months until he was pronounced cured, and he eventually grew into a tall, straight young chap. Later, I helped them with the threshing, standing on the rick as it got higher and higher, wondering how I would ever get down, and I was there the day that the bull put Arthur up a tree … Yes, the outdoor life was getting its hold on me, and I revelled in it, being paid one shilling (5p) an hour plus a sack of corn for my mother's hens.

My brother named some of the hens after various relations whom he disliked. This made it easier for us to eat them. Sometimes we had one of the older hens for Sunday lunch, and he would enquire, "Is this Cousin Phoebe?" (She was really a very nice person – I don't know why he disliked her so much) and on being told that indeed it was, he would consume her with great relish.

The year was 1947, and my mother, who loved to entertain, was still gathering her many cousins together, rediscovering them after not seeing them throughout the war, and inviting them for weekends. Her grandmother had 12 children, hence the abundance of cousins.

John, after studying Arabic in the POW camp, had joined the Sudan

Political Service, following in the footsteps of our illustrious great-great-uncle, General Charles Gordon, and happened to be on three months' leave.

He became rather rebellious about being on parade for all these aunts, uncles and cousins. So much so, that one morning, when my mother announced at breakfast the impending arrival of yet another cousin (female), he declared that he did not want to meet her at the station and was "going to Chichester to buy a gun". (Not, I hasten to add, that he intended to *shoot* this unknown cousin; he just needed a gun to take to the Sudan.)

Our mother duly arrived at the station to meet her favourite cousin's daughter, a medical student, but as the train drew in, she noticed John and his friend Robert skulking behind some milk churns on the platform. Before she could reach the cousin to greet her, the boys had got there first, shaking hands, carrying her cases and being most affable. Curiosity had won the day and they couldn't resist taking a look, and having taken it, couldn't resist speaking to her!

All that weekend they never left her side. Picnics, swimming in the river, walks on the common … John was completely bowled over. Six weeks later he became engaged to his second cousin, Mary Shaw. Her father was Chief Surgeon for North Devon and the head of five partners in a practice in Barnstaple. There were a few anxious telephone calls between Sussex and Devon on the subject of cousins marrying, but the verdict was that it was All Right.

Sadly, before those six weeks were up and the engagement announced, my father died. There had been one ghastly weekend when he and I had both been ill: he bellowing with pain, and I sick after nearly drowning in the river and swallowing what seemed like several pints of slimy river water. Robert had been giving me a swimming lesson and had let go of me, thinking that I would swim naturally. I didn't. That time, we both recovered, but there came a morning which I will never forget.

DEATH

I GOT UP EARLY AND WENT DOWNSTAIRS TO clean the dining-room, because it was my turn. There are not many 17-year-olds nowadays who either rise at that hour *or* do any cleaning, and I should explain how this came about. When we were small, however hard-up our parents were, the presence of a charwoman ever hoovered in the background. Over the years, it has become fashionable to call these 'treasures' by various names, from 'Mrs Mop' to 'the cleaning woman' – rather derogatory and mostly used by men – or 'My Daily' (who is more likely to be weekly). My favourite is The Woman Who *Does*. In our time we had progressed from Mrs Whybrow, who was Irish, unnaturally red-haired, called our mother 'Meddim' and spat her cigarette into the washing-up whenever she heard anyone approaching, to Rose, who was six foot four with a very short haircut and incredibly long, ungainly legs that seemed to lean sideways so that she resembled a lamp post which had been knocked into in the night. Anything less like a rose would be hard to find, unless her parents had named her after Rosa Gigantea, which grows to 30 feet. She was also clumsy, and broke things. My father had christened her 'the Elephant'. When it was Rose's day for cleaning, he hid all his belongings, 'in case the Elephant treads on them' …

Recently, however, one of my aunts had pointed out to my mother that there was no need for expenditure on cleaners when she had three able-bodied teenagers in the house (myself and the two cousins who were brought up with us). Very unwillingly, we were organised into taking turns to 'do' the downstairs rooms before breakfast and the upstairs rooms *after* breakfast.

It was therefore my turn to be cleaning the dining-room when I heard my father call …

He was calling from the study, where he slept since he could no longer get up the stairs. To my eternal shame, I did not go immediately, partly because I wanted to finish what I was doing and partly because he had a habit of 'crying wolf', causing one to abandon the task in hand only to find that he didn't really want anything. So I let him go on shouting while

I finished the cleaning and laid the breakfast table. For the rest of my life I felt too terrible to think about this.

When I went to him, he asked me to fetch my mother, and he looked very ill. She rushed downstairs, telling me to fetch my brother, but as she entered the room, my father looked at her and fell back. For once, the doctor came in double-quick time, but there was nothing he could do. John came into the dining-room and said, "He has gone." I felt overcome with guilt for not having gone to him at once, although nobody could have saved him unless he had been in hospital. I always managed to do the wrong thing. Hating housework, I had been trying to get the tedious task over as soon as possible, without interruption. Now, my father would never be able to interrupt me again. He had always been devoted to me: we had the same interests – gardening, painting and drawing, writing and languages – but my affection for him had been rather mixed up by the fact that he and my mother were not happy together, so I suffered from divided loyalties.

The Stationmaster's wife arrived, her dark hair flowing wildly loose, and shut herself into the study to lay out my father. This was her part-time career. When she had finished, we accepted, reluctantly, her invitation to look at him.

I have always wished that I hadn't, but it was the thing to do in those days: each friend or relation who came to the house to offer condolences was asked if he or she would like 'to see him'. Surprisingly, they all did.

The face that I saw was completely unfamiliar. It haunted me for months, and I saw it in dreams. Peaceful, I suppose, but not my Daddy. Thinking painfully back to it now, he looked *young* again, and I had never seen him young ...

On the outskirts of our village lived a charming couple, who visited the 'Swan Inn' regularly and made friends with my parents. The wife was a niece of the Queen and the husband was a Major in the Coldstream Guards. 'The Queen's niece', as she was called by the villagers, shattered all the snobs and social climbers by playing Shove-Ha'penny with the plumber in the Public Bar. My father had been very taken with her, and used to send me up to her cottage on my bike with presents of vegetables from his garden. Sadly, she had tuberculosis, and her husband took her away to a sanatorium in Switzerland, where she died a few weeks before my father. She was only 34.

Her husband had come home utterly grief-stricken and inconsolable, but when he heard of my father's death he was one of the first to come round and commiserate with my mother and offer help with the funeral arrangements. Despite his grief, he had a wonderful sense of humour and could not resist a chuckle at his own incompetence when he returned from ordering flowers for his wife's grave and my father's funeral, and told us that he had accidentally backed his car into the florist's shop window and smashed it.

"What a laugh for my wife and your father in Heaven," he said, "when they see that I smashed the window getting flowers for them!"

It was the first funeral I had ever been to, and I managed not to break down (a friend described my expression as 'dignified') but all the time I was haunted by guilt, and by that dead face which had so startled me.

The Lord's in the Garden

Our family had dwindled to two, and my mother and I found it very quiet on our own. John had returned to the Sudan after announcing his engagement, to the fury of many mothers who had hoped that his attentions to their daughters meant more than they did. Mary returned to do one more year at a hospital in London to complete her studies and become a surgeon. The wedding was planned for the following spring.

I could not leave my mother alone in the house, and I needed a proper job. The people at the Riding School came to the rescue: they were in the habit of employing girls to groom the horses, muck out the stables, weed the garden and, worst of all, because I was not tall enough, *catch* the horses, which entailed hours of endless pursuit, halter in hand, as very few of them were obliging enough to stop and put their heads down while I reached up and secured the halter. For this I got 10 shillings (50p) a week and a free ride whenever I wanted one.

So, I drifted into a routine of helping (or not helping) my mother in the mornings (she looked after people's babies while the mothers were working or taking a holiday, and sometimes we had up to four toddlers at a time) and pedalling up to the stables in the afternoons.

In the evenings and at weekends if we were free, our one source of local entertainment was to go round to the pub to hear the latest village gossip, of which there was always plenty, and it was usually fairly riveting. While my mother indulged in one glass of sherry, and I in innocuous lemonade, we learned that somebody's 15-year-old son had managed to make his 13-year-old sister pregnant, that the cowman's daughter had been seen rolling in the hay with the builder's son, etc., etc.

All this fascinating information was whispered across the bar by the prim-looking barmaid with her grey, pudding-basin haircut, who always had a large cup of tea in front of her and claimed never to have tasted any of the alcoholic drinks which she purveyed.

Many of our friends packed out that little bar, and it was the great meeting-place of the village, a lot of witty conversation flowing in competition with the ale, which, we were told, tasted disgusting because they didn't keep the barrels the right way up.

In the winter, village dances, or 'hops', were the greatest fun, but there was a great deal of social climbing and snobbery about private entertainment. I did not get invited to the dances and parties in the houses of the rich. We had no money, no *car* (*very* much a status symbol) and, worst of all, no longer a spare, eligible *man* ... and, of course, I wore spectacles ... Bearing in mind that my mother's parents had lived in something akin to a palace in India, and that her father, but for his untimely death, might have been the next Viceroy, I think she could have been forgiven for feeling a bit sore about this. However, one evening when she was feeling particularly hurt at not being invited to a party at the house of someone who considered himself the 'Squire' of the village, we went round to the 'Swan' for consolation and began airing our grievances to the sympathetic barmaid. The only other occupant of the Private Bar was the Queen's nephew, who was staying with his brother-in-law. "Aren't you going to the party?" we asked.

"Oh, no," he said, "They're *much* too snobbish to ask *me!*" We felt much better.

However, I continued to feel strong sympathy for my mother, the penniless widow of a dashing Cavalry Major, being alternately ignored, looked down on or patronised by a lot of jumped-up, nouveau-riche people with very affected voices, but for myself I didn't really mind, as I hated smart parties, never knew what to say to the well-groomed young men, and was horribly conscious of my spectacles, which ruined everything. If I didn't wear them, I couldn't see the eyes and facial expressions of the people to whom I was talking. You need to be able to see if you are boring someone, or if they are appreciating your humour ... My brothers had ordered me not to speak unless I had anything interesting to say. I never considered that anything I had to say was interesting, so I seldom spoke. Ten years later, the invention of contact lenses was to change my life ...

A few days later, the Queen's nephew invited me to tea at his brother-in-law's cottage. I was really rather infatuated with the brother-in-law, 20 years older than I was, but he was anxious to arrange an alliance, or, in the vernacular, 'get me off' with Lord G—, who was a problem to him, as he was not quite mentally stable (he did have a brain operation which improved things, but the brother-in-law found it irksome having to be his keeper).

That afternoon, I arrived at the charming, cream-washed cottage in time for tea, and was greeted at the gate by the gardener, who rejoiced in the name of Underdone. Rather Biblically, he announced in sepulchral tones, "The Lord's in the garden." We sat at a small table on the lawn, opposite each other, the Lord and I, and both being painfully shy, struggled with polite conversation about nothing much.

Being the youngest of my family, I was not in the habit of pouring out the tea, but, just in time, I realised that this was required of me here. The brothers-in-law contributed quite a lot to our meagre social life at that time, frequently causing us much amusement when they came round to sit in our house after closing time while they waited for a taxi to take them home when they had slightly overindulged. The Lord's brain trouble meant that it took very little alcohol to make his legs collapse.

'Aunt Elizabeth' rang frequently from the Palace to enquire after her nephew's welfare. The telephone exchange was manned by a wonderful character called Mr Cooper, who listened to all conversations, as far as we could gather, for if my mother asked to be put through to a certain friend, Mr Cooper would say, "Oh, it's no good ringing *her* – she's having tea with Mrs X." He ruled the whole village, really, and people were far too terrified to make late night calls, in case they got Mr Cooper out of bed. He would certainly have told them off if they had. However, he had to make an exception for the Queen, although he would rather cheekily announce that 'Aunt Elizabeth' was on the line.

A Swiss male nurse with a hedgehog haircut was employed to keep an eye on the Lord, and proceeded to pursue me wherever I went, even when his nose was in splints after a disagreement with one of his employers, but eventually His (but not, after all, *my*) Lordship returned to Scotland and inherited the Earldom on the death of his father. The rightful heir, his eldest brother, had been killed in the war.

The brother-in-law became a barrister and later married one of his late wife's bridesmaids. They had two sons and lived happily ever after. I was rather sad at the time, but there were to be plenty more objects of my unrequited love before I found The Right One.

From Mucking Out to Planting Out

EIGHTEEN MONTHS OF THE DEAD-END JOB AT the Riding Stables were quite enough and, after much conflicting advice on careers from well-meaning friends and relations, accompanied by a lot of "You are wasting your education" I decided to follow in the footsteps of one of my brother's ex-girlfriends and train as a gardener at the local Stately Home. She had gone from there to Reading University to obtain a degree in Horticulture.

My interview with the Head Gardener took place in a summerhouse, where we sat side by side – unlike the traditional encounter when one faces the prospective employer across a desk. He was rather a weird character, super-intelligent, who had written more than a dozen gardening books, but had a giant chip on his shoulder.

I was assigned to the greenhouses under the care and instruction of an extremely knowledgeable ex-sailor, who had an endless repertoire of popular songs which he whistled continuously, changing smoothly from one to another, like a pianist playing a medley. The tune that particularly reminds me of him is *Red Roses for a Blue Lady*.

My first day was spent scrubbing 300 flowerpots. Every time the Head Gardener passed me, he said, "We all have to start at the bottom, you know." I had difficulty in convincing him that I never expected to start anywhere else. I was quite taken aback when one of the young gardeners asked me, as we scrubbed our boots in the horse-trough before going home, whether my mother had "butlers and things". I didn't bother to point out that I would hardly be working there for £3 per fortnight if she did!

Mr Whitehead liked to tell everyone that he had trained the man who was now Head Gardener at Buckingham Palace. This was an individual called Fred Nutbeam. One day, when George Whitehead was going to a publisher's cocktail party in London, to launch one of his many gardening books, he decided to invite Fred to go with him. A very condescending individual looked down his nose at Fred (who probably wasn't wearing the right kind of suit, if a suit at all) and asked, "Who do you write for?" Fred replied that he didn't write, he was just a gardener. The conversation then ran more or less as follows:-

"Oh and where is your garden?"

"London," replied Fred.

"On the outskirts, I suppose."

"No," said Fred, "it's in Victoria."

"Victoria! It can't be very large …"

"Just about 49 acres," announced Fred, calmly.

"Ridiculous," snapped his interrogator; "there couldn't be a garden of that size in Victoria – I don't believe a word of it," and away he swept.

Throughout the party, Fred continued to keep everyone guessing, and never let on that he was Head Gardener of Buckingham Palace.

"Remember," said Mr Whitehead to me on that first day, "you are being taught by the chap who taught the Head Gardener of Buckingham Palace gardens, and tell all your friends …"

My second most tedious job was potting up several thousand tomato seedlings which we supplied to the Fulham Allotment Holders. It took us three weeks to complete the order and, to amuse ourselves, we played 20 questions until we became so telepathic that each could guess what the other was thinking in only one question…

At Christmas time, every member of the staff – gardeners, foresters, builders, maintenance men, domestic staff, you name them – received a bonus of – wait for it – three shillings (15p) in a tiny brown envelope. I found John, my workmate, looking very serious: "I have a terrible decision to make," he said. "Shall I spend it on two new buttons for my overalls, or a Mars bar?"

The two years that I spent in Parham Gardens (one in the greenhouses and one outside) were full of fun and laughter, as well as an excellent training, which has been useful all my life. The foreman, George Searle, taught me always to tackle the hardest job first, and to start at the farthest end of the row, so that when you are tired you only have the easy jobs left, and the shortest way to go. I have applied this to everything. When you are old, this simple discipline becomes not only useful, but vital!

I endured endless leg-pulling and listened to brilliantly witty repartee in the potting shed. When, for my six-mile journey before 7.30 a.m., I graduated from a pushbike to an autocycle with L-plates, the men used to leap off their bikes and rush up the nearest tree in mock terror when they heard me coming … They were all great characters and I enjoyed hearing their views on politics. If their arguments became really heated, the other Land-Girl would say to me, "Let's get out of the 'ouse of Commons before the blood runs under the door!"

They not only taught me about gardening – they taught me about Life.

However, I never went to Reading University, because my brother and his wife invited me to go out to the Sudan and look after their children, and this was too good a chance to miss, which proved to be another of my most happy experiences (described in a separate book, *To the Sun and Back*).

When I returned from that vast country with its wonderfully hospitable people, where I had made many friends, I was dithering once more over what to do next when a friend happened to mention that she was going to do an interesting secretarial course in London, which included Journalism and Commercial French, and suggested that we should go together and share a bedsitter or something. I was now over 21 and could use part of my grandmother's legacy to pay for the course. My mother didn't want me to leave home again, but I realised that, once I had this training behind me, I would be able to get a job anywhere: secretarial jobs were to be had all over London at that time and quite highly paid.

Typing to the Teddy Bears' Picnic

THE 'IN' PLACE TO LEARN SECRETARIAL SKILLS in the 'fifties was the Triangle Secretarial College, run by three women whose initials were T, J and S (Miss Thompson, Miss Jenkins and Miss Stranack) and these letters also stood for Typewriting, Journalism and Shorthand. You paid by the month, and the full course lasted for nine months, but if you managed to qualify and were accepted in a job, you could leave after six months.

Being there was very good for our figures, as we spent a great deal of time running up and down stairs to different classes. Studying Shorthand with Miss Mossop, who was a Margaret Rutherford lookalike, was a big laugh, and we ended up *dreaming* in shorthand at night.

There was a new intake of girls every fortnight. Typing was done on ancient typewriters – some from the 1890s – to music, very slowly and jerkily, starting with *The Teddy-Bears' Picnic* and progressing to hot jazz as we became more proficient. This music was played on scratchy gramophone records and was said to help us to type evenly. When we were considered sufficiently competent, the College found us a job, in which we were entreated to stay for at least six months, or, better still, a year, so that it would look good on a reference – i.e., showing that you were a stayer rather than a fly-by-night.

As we set out for that first interview, the main advice given was: 'Don't forget to *smile*.' This was easier said than done if you were feeling sick with nerves.

Instead of getting a flat on our own, we went to a club for young people, which was the Headquarters of all the Youth Clubs in Britain. They gave us rather strange things for breakfast, such as spaghetti on toast, and we paid extra for an evening meal if we were not going out anywhere. This was more likely to be *beans* on toast, preceded by thin soup and followed by rice-pudding or tinned fruit and custard. We discovered a taxi-drivers' cafe down the road, where we could get fish and chips, a slice of bread-and-butter and a cup of tea for one shilling altogether. No tip required…

At the Club there was a small electric fire in each room, which cost one shilling an hour in the meter if you had only one bar on, and two shillings for both bars. We hurried to get our shorthand homework done before the

120

meter ran out, after which we either got into bed in our dressing-gowns, or went to the cinema to keep warm in the ninepenny seats (right up against the screen, so that everything looked distorted). We walked about a mile to the Triangle every morning. At lunchtime we competed to see who could find the cheapest lunch. Once, I succeeded in winning this trial of restraint and obligatory self-control at the ABC Café (there was a whole chain of them all over London; whatever happened to them, I wonder?), spending 10½d (about 4p) on a meat pie, beans, mash and some watery orange squash.

For interviews it was vital to be without ladders in our stockings. It seems unbelievable now, but tights as we know them were not yet available, only thick, probably 30-denier, tights could be obtained in bright blue, green, or red.

I claim to have been the first to think of proper tights, as I was constantly moaning, "Why can't they make *stocking*-coloured tights?"

Some of the girls didn't need to worry about the interviews, as they were going to work for 'Daddy', or 'Daddy's friend', but I was getting short of money, and needed to earn some. After six-and-a-half months, they sent me for an interview with a small advertising agency, where I was confronted by a large man with a beard and an ear-trumpet, who barked, "How much money do you want?" I had not been prepared for this; usually employers advertised the amount that they were prepared to pay, so, very cautiously, I replied, "What do you think I am worth?" This was greeted with loud shouts of laughter, making me feel like a slave in a market.

The princely sum of five pounds 10 shillings a week was arrived at, and the following Monday I trudged from High Holborn station to Lincoln's Inn Fields. It was a strange place for an advertising agency, as all the other companies in the building were law firms. I worked in a dingy brown room, typing on buff-coloured paper with a dingy brown letter-heading, in company with a bright young spark aged 17, called Sheila, from Hornchurch who apparently spent her free time having rows with her boyfriend – almost every morning, she bounced in, saying, "Guess wot – we've 'ad a row!" – and an older redhead who had been engaged for 12 years and was still saving up for her 'bottom drawer'.

They warned me not to go near the Art Department, as all the artists were "mad for it". The copywriters were more respectable (two male, one female) and all married.

We advertised earthmoving equipment, trailers and tractors, and SALT! Sifta Sam the Salt Man had been invented by the Bearded One who had interviewed me and it was his proudest achievement. Inexplicably, he occasionally made assignations with me to meet for a Sunday morning drink at the 'Dove', by the Thames at Hammersmith. By that time I was, as one of my friends described it, "living with the Vicar" – I was actually renting a room in a Vicarage in Fulham Palace Road for £1 per week, from which I got a trolley-bus to Hammersmith and a tube to High Holborn.

Through Stevens Advertising Service, in an indirect sort of way, I met a girl who had worked for the *Daily Mail*. Learning that Fleet Street was my ultimate goal, she got me an interview. This was after I had endured the dingy brown office for nine months (almost enough to please Miss T, Miss J and Miss S at the Triangle).

At Northcliffe House I faced the most terrifying interview yet, with a tall, dark, curly-moustached, Spanish-looking man who completely threw me by enquiring, "Why do you particularly want to work for the *Weekend Mail*?"

I had to think quickly: I had been given to understand that it was the *Daily Mail*, but some sixth sense warned me that it would be tactless to say so.

"Oh, *any* newspaper will do – I have always wanted to be in Fleet Street," I replied eagerly, putting my foot right *in* it; the *Weekend Mail* was his pride and joy, and he thought I had selected it as rising above all others! I had not even *seen* a copy, but was told that it was a rival to the Mirror group's highly popular tabloid newspaper, *Reveille*.

Friends advised me to take the job, to get my foot in the door of Northcliffe House, and to keep my eyes open for better opportunities within Associated Newspapers as and when they should arise. Later, I learned that my new, Spanish-looking editor's family was connected with Carreras Cigars …

The paper, which had evolved from the forces *Overseas Mail*, was manned by an interesting crowd of characters, and was hilariously funny (mostly unintentionally) with its trashy stories about showbiz 'stars' and footballers. On the telephone it was hard for us to believe that we were actually talking to these people; on one occasion I heard one of the secretaries say, "Well, if you're Benny Hill, I'm Marilyn Monroe," only to turn scarlet the next minute as she realised that he really *was* Benny Hill!

We spent a lot of time replying to the readers' letters, many of which were written on the backs of sugar-bags, butchers' bills and wrapping paper. I shared an office with the Agony Column and Women's Fashions, the latter of whom sat typing in a red velour hat. They discussed all the problems which were sent to the Agony Column by desperate women, and some of these made one's hair stand on end. One family in particular seemed to be in such a sexual predicament that we wondered if the letter was a leg-pull. On the backs of several blue Tate & Lyle sugar-bags, a young girl wrote to tell us that her mother was sleeping with her sister's boyfriend, her father was sleeping with *her*, her brother slept in the bath, and so on, until the whole family's life seemed to be one long, incestuous orgy – What Should She Do About It?

The prim and proper Agony Column, grey hair strained back in a bun, decided that somebody might easily be taking the Mickey, and as there seemed to be no possible answer, wisely ignored it. Sometimes, men wrote passionate letters, professing to have fallen in love with *her* – just by reading her kind replies ...

We secretaries, or 'Editorial Assistants' as we were called (in fact, I was described as 'aide, organiser and *nurse*' to the Features Editor) had to join the NATSOPA printers' union, while journalists had to join the NUJ, and to do this they had to prove that they earned a certain amount per annum from their writing. It was really a closed shop, because there seemed no way for a beginner to break in if nobody would give them any writing to do ...

We were forced to attend NATSOPA union meetings, and fined if we didn't. One girl used to take her knitting, as these meetings were incredibly boring. A man who was called the Father of the Chapel used to address us as 'Brothers' and proceed to spout the longest words in the dictionary, ad infinitum, *exactly* like Peter Sellers in *I'm All Right, Jack*. (Peter Sellers must have attended a similar meeting to get it so true to form.)

I understood that a proportion of our Union subs went to the Labour Party, but was informed that, if I wished, I could 'opt out'. This I did, not only because I had been dragooned at home by the local retired Brigadier into being Secretary of the Young Conservatives, but because I was a great admirer of Harold Macmillan, and agreed with him that We Had Never Had It So Good ... However, I must admit that I was very grateful to the Union for ensuring that we were extremely well paid. My graduate friends from the Triangle, in ordinary secretarial jobs (not newspapers) were earning £6 per week, whereas I started at £8.8s a week, rising to £10. Even so, living in London, travelling home to the country at weekends, and giving my mother £1 per week (my brother gave her much more) did not leave much over – and we had to be smartly dressed.

When we had started earning, we had moved out of the Club and into bedsitters or shared flats. My weekly rent (for a bedsitter in a house full of friends, including the Wing-Commander (Selby-Lowndes) who started Securicor, was 35 shillings (£1.75) and the rest of my earnings, distributed on Fridays in a small, brown paper packet, were divided into envelopes marked 'Food', 'Fares', 'Clothes' and, hopefully, 'Anything Over', which usually remained empty.

Most of us entered the office on Friday mornings with a halfpenny as our sole capital, so woe betide us if the pay packets came round *after* lunch. Sometimes, to be forearmed, I took a sandwich with me on a Friday, just in case. That is, if I had anything left to put in a sandwich.

There was a way of supplementing our incomes: we could volunteer for overtime, which meant double pay for every hour worked during the evening.

This usually consisted of dealing with entries when the paper had been running a competition. Several huge laundry baskets of entries would be brought in, and we had to open them and sort them all out. A tedious job, but it was very exciting to be at the hub of a big national daily at night, especially when a big news story had broken, such as a murder, and 100 typewriters were clattering away at full speed, tea slopping in saucers as reporters, some with hats on, rushed to get their stories completed. It was thrilling just to be there.

On one occasion we had promised the readers that if they each filled in a coupon and sent us a shilling, they could have a piece of one of Frankie Vaughan's suits. He was the pop-idol of the time. A very amusing girl called Midge, who had been given the task of cutting up the suit and sending off the snippets, burst into our room dramatically saying, "I can't make up my mind who's going to be the lucky one to get the flies!"

There was another letters page called Uncle George's Column. Readers wrote stupid letters to which 'Uncle George', who was really a defrocked admiral (so I was told) wrote fatuous jokes in reply. On Fridays (pay day) he got drunk and stuffed the nearest secretary head-first into the wastepaper basket. Even I suffered this indignity once, when, forgetting what day it was, I had to go into his room, which he shared with various writers, one of whom was the famous David English, who eventually became Editor of the *Daily Mail*. He was then aged 25, and used to bribe me with boiled sweets whenever he wanted a letter typed. The Agony Column used to remark, quite rightly, "David will go far, one day."

I supposed I could have stayed there indefinitely without a care in the world, laughing my way through life, but I wanted something better, and my family certainly wanted me to 'get away from that dreadful little rag'. Two friends on the *Daily Mail* (which was on the same floor, although we were tucked away along a side corridor) told me that there was a vacancy in *Daily Mail* Features; the Features Editor's ancient secretary was retiring. Features covered almost everything that wasn't actually News, i.e., book reviews, film reviews, music, art, articles by famous writers and politicians, even the crosswords and cartoons.

My prospective boss was just about as shy as I was, but we blushed and mumbled our way through the interview, and he told me that my most important task would be to prevent people from speaking to him on the telephone. I was to say that he was "In Conference". He was to spend the next five years 'In Conference' while I stammered rather untruthful excuses into the telephone to lots of famous (and some infamous) people …

FLEET STREET

ALMOST FIVE YEARS SPED BY, AS I was fully occupied, performing a wide variety of tasks, all punctuated by constant telephone calls. Apart from answering a few letters each day, I did surprisingly little typing. When I look back on it, I see myself running around the editorial floor on various errands, summoning journalists to 'come and have a word with Mac', the Features Editor, and being sent up two floors to the printers in what was called the 'Composing Room', carrying a mock-up of the day-after-tomorrow's feature page, on which was written something that looked like 'Frying Tonight', but was, in fact, 'Flong Tonight'. (Flong, in journalistic slang, means 'material that is not urgently topical'.)

On the way back, I would enjoy a bit of badinage and Cockney repartee with the jokers in the Tape Room. This was a small, open-fronted room full of shuddering machines, jumping up and down as they spewed long messages in capital letters from all over the world: sort of precursors to telex and fax machines, I imagine. If there was something of interest to our department, it would be handed to me. Making a slight detour, I might pass through the Sports department, where Harry Carpenter, the famous boxing correspondent, was always ready for a friendly chat. The whole floor was open-plan, but with glass partitions, so that we could wave to each other while talking on the telephone. Mac complained that it felt like being in a goldfish bowl.

From the canteen on the third floor, I fetched disgusting cups of coffee for my boss and the sub-editors. The canteen tea was even more revolting, tasting like a mixture of acorns and washing-up water; maybe it was. The food, some of which was still rationed at that time, was unspeakable, but we had all got used to eating very plain food during the war.

Most of us preferred to go out of the building during the lunch hour. The 'Wig & Pen' was a popular place for lunch, but took rather too long for us to get back within the hour. The 'Kardomah Café' (another chain which disappeared), in Chancery Lane, was self-service, and therefore quicker, and I used to meet a friend who worked for a barrister. We observed two men who lunched there every single day, one of whom became known as 'the egg-on-toast man', because he told us that he had been having a poached egg on toast at this café every day for 27 years! What on earth must his cholesterol count have been?!

Soon, at the opposite end of Fleet Street, a new, vegetarian health food place started up, supplying salads of all kinds, with mountains of grated carrot, for which we all queued.

My boss was keen to have controversial and interesting writers on his page, and when they came in to discuss their articles I sat and listened. Two feet away from the great and the brilliant, I drank it all in with awe. Bernard Levin (whose appearance disappointed me terribly), Alan Brien, Marshall Pugh and many others all graced our little office. One of the most charming was the film critic, Fred Majdalany, whose wife also charmed me when she rang up, asking me to remind him to bring her such items as 'a jar of paprika' on his way home. From the sublime to the ridiculous, I once had to accompany a known criminal to the Cashiers, to be paid for 'his side of the story'. There were two brothers, Alfred and Albert Hinds, and I can't remember which of the two it was, but it gave me a kick!

Leslie Illingworth, in my opinion the greatest political cartoonist of all time, who has not had nearly enough recognition, had a studio on the top floor of Northcliffe House; the floor which housed the *Sunday Dispatch*. Once a week, he drew a full-page cartoon for *Punch*, and attended 'Punch Lunch', which they had every Wednesday. However, the great man, a Welshman who had started selling cartoons to Cardiff papers while still at school, had one failing: he was slow to get going, and frequently, when the time was near for the cartoon to be wired to the Scottish Edition, which went to press earlier than our Southern Editions, my boss would send me upstairs 'to see how Leslie is getting on'.

I would find Leslie Illingworth seated in front of a completely blank page! No wonder Mac had white hair at the age of 43! Sometimes the cartoon would then be executed, brilliantly and with amazing rapidity. At other times, however, a photograph of Highland cattle would have to be substituted in the Scottish Edition …

One day, my boss came in with a purposeful look on his face: "I want to find an artist called Moira Hoddell," he said. "I like her work and we need a resident artist to illustrate various items on the features pages." He disappeared to the reference library, to look up cuttings of her recent work and try to track her down.

Moira had drawn a middle-page spread of the entire Coronation procession in 1953, and her drawings for tourists, of London sights to see, were attached to all the bus stops, while already her pictures had hung at the Royal Academy of Arts Summer Exhibitions – noted in Tanfield's 1952 Diary.

Her arrival at the *Daily Mail* was the start of a long friendship with me, as she breezed into our office with her ideas, full of *joie-de-vivre* and lively laughter. One of her tasks was to illustrate the radio programmes on the back page, and I still remember her portrayal of *Woman's Hour* as a huge bride with a satisfied smirk on her face, dragging a tiny little man down the aisle!

Illingworth shared his studio with her, and I found excuses to nip up there and share their laughter whenever I could. It was not uncommon to hear whistled strains from *La Traviata* echoing down the corridor of the sixth floor as Moira tramped towards the Picture Library. Here were photographs of all the reporters (with whom I was constantly falling in love – all one-sided) and Moira sympathetically pinched the odd photograph for me to cherish under my pillow!

This idyllic, exciting, fun-filled life could have gone on for ever, had it not been for one of these romantic obsessions becoming two-sided for a short time and then breaking up when I discovered that he was not just two-timing me, but probably four- or five-timing me, and seeing him every day in the office became unbearable. Also, I wasn't really getting anywhere with my ambition to write. Although I had experienced the excitement of having my first article printed on one of the feature pages, shortly followed by another, no one had answered my plea to join the reporting staff. 'Too much Union Trouble,' they predicted.

I don't think my first article would ever have appeared in the paper – or even been written – had it not been for the help and encouragement of an excitable little part-Russian journalist called Olga Franklin, who had recently joined us from the *Daily Sketch*. We shared the same sense of humour, and she would always stop to chat with me when passing en route for the Library, her high-pitched giggle echoing all over the Editorial floor when I told her some piece of internal gossip. She could even make a short memo sound funny, and would always leave notes to say where she had gone – for example, *"Jo: Have gone to see Chicken Farmer with callouses on his thumb!"* …what news story this led to, I can't recall – but I kept the memo.

The idea for my article started with a practical joke: Olga had been writing a series of slimming articles for a couple of weeks, which caused me to complain to my friends, "Every paper you pick up has slimming articles on the woman's page, and I am so sick of reading them – I'm skinny, and they never have *fattening* articles …"

That night, at midnight, in a euphoric state after being taken to see The Crazy Gang at the Victoria Palace, I sat down at the kitchen table and wrote a leg-pull: a 'How-Can-I, Miss Franklin, Look-Like-You-Once-Looked?' type article, intended only for Olga's eyes, and the next morning, quietly placed it on her desk, slightly wondering whether she would think it too cheeky …

Imagine my amazement and delight when Olga erupted into our office, screaming to the Features Editor and Deputy Editor, Bill Hardcastle, who happened to be in the room, "You've *got* to print this, you've just *got* to!"

They did! It was my first time ever in print (apart from *Time & Tide* and *Spectator* competitions) – and in a National Daily! The thrill was almost too much for me … I shall never forget it, and it was all due to Olga, pushing the men to print it; I never had the courage of my convictions, or that push that a journalist requires. Some of the great writers of the day congratulated me, although there was one disagreeable character who said that someone must have written it for me, as I did not look capable, etc., etc.

It didn't stop there: the *Daily Mail* decided to run a series of fattening articles, with me as the guinea pig and Olga deciding what I should eat, giving reports on my daily progress. Cartoons appeared, of Olga feeding me with an outsize spoon. We never stopped laughing, and at the end of the week I weighed *exactly the same*! Olga said that it would be funnier if we said that I had *lost* a pound, so we did. She always knew how to make a story have that little twist of expertise at the end.

I have never known anyone who worked so hard: she did Russian broadcasts for the BBC (also translations) and she wrote several books, apart from her regular reporting for the *Daily Mail*, going anywhere they chose to send her. We always kept in touch by letter, although I never actually saw her again after leaving the *Mail*. Her letters were full of intentions to come over and see us, but always her car broke down, or was stolen, or some other disaster prevented her from coming. Many years later, when we were going through a bad patch financially, she came to the rescue by giving me a lot of work to do, researching two of her books. Olga paid me over-generously, undoubtedly far more than I deserved, and even sent money to my children at Christmas, although she had never met them. (My husband had been made redundant at the age of 49, and all prospective employers were treating him as if he were 99.)

Olga carried on working right into her seventies, announcing cheerfully in one of her last letters, *'I have had <u>three</u> unsuccessful major operations and one minor one, but I manage to keep going because I need the money to keep my handicapped brother and other relatives …'* She was a childless widow and all her family seemed to depend on her. When I listened to her last BBC interview before her inevitable death from cancer, I got the impression that Death, to her, was going to be just another interesting assignment.

Woman's Hour was kind enough to read out my tribute to her,

Olga's Memo:
If Mr Aitken wants me, please will you tell him dear that I
have gone to see the chicken-farm – man-with-callouses-on-his-
thumb at Framfield, Sussex this morning.

Apart from the (romantic) reason already given, a combination of events was responsible for my decision to leave the *Mail*. A new Editor had arrived, and he had brought with him several of his colleagues from another paper, placing them in all the top jobs and ruthlessly throwing out existing staff, who had been there for 20 years or more. Sadly, one of the casualties was 'Mac' – Charles Mackinnon, my Features Editor boss, who had 10 times the talent, experience and wit of the newcomer, even having written for *Punch* in years gone by, but his shy, modest personality was, alas, no match for the new, ruthless young Editor. Suddenly, it was the Age of Youth Culture – everyone, it seemed, had to be under 35, and anyone with the wisdom of long experience was thrown on the scrap heap.

Poor Mac was relegated to being just a sub-editor, taking orders from a 30-year-old who turned out to be the Wrong Man! It was a complete Evelyn Waugh *Scoop* scenario. (For non-readers of Evelyn Waugh, this was the story of a *Nature Notes* man being sent in error to cover a tribal war in some obscure Middle-Eastern country.) Someone had noticed that the *Evening Standard* was carrying excellent features, and they had promptly 'poached' the *Standard*'s Features Editor, a common practice in Fleet Street. Too late, they had discovered that it was his Deputy who had all the bright ideas … It took them many months to right this wrong, finally succeeding in removing the one and replacing him with the other. The Deputy would have been a wonderful person for me to work with, but by this time I had moved myself to another department (very dull) working for Special Correspondents, one of whom caused me to type an average of 27 letters per day, thanking no one in particular for his Press handouts!

As we finished work quite late – our hours were 10 a.m. to 6.00 p.m. and we seldom left on the dot – social life consisted mainly of a drink or two in the 'Feathers', the 'Mucky Duck', which was next door, or 'Auntie's' which, I think, was the 'Rose & Crown'. I once met George Melly and Wally Fawkes in there with Leslie Illingworth, and Wally took out his clarinet and began to play, whereupon George Melly seized me and danced up and down the very small floor space in the bar. A brief brush with the famous!

On one of these slightly drunken evenings, we ended up having borscht soup made by the Finnish girlfriend of a Features sub-editor called Rae Hopkins, known as 'Hoppy', in his flat (or possibly hers). It was the first time that most of us had been introduced to this soup, which was accompanied by black bread. Hoppy tipped the scales for me: "If you stay in this job much longer, you'll turn into 'Our Miss Snooks who's been with us 30 years'," he teased. "You keep moaning about not being allowed to be a reporter, not finding a husband, not getting any … Why don't you go and see the world, do some interesting jobs and write about them?!"

"That's it," I said, defiantly, "I'm running away to sea!"

This unexpected announcement had been prompted by a magazine article which I had read while under the dryer at the hairdresser's. It was all about jobs for girls as Assistant Pursers on ocean liners. The old *Queen Mary* and *Queen Elizabeth* each had Pursers' staffs of 25 in all, nine of whom were girls. They typed the ship's manifests, crew-lists (perhaps I typed John Prescott's name, but as there were 1,200 crew I don't remember), accident reports for the ship's hospital – if a passenger overbalanced in rough seas and broke ribs, or a limb, it all had to be recorded on a form – and a passenger could ask for a lady purser to take shorthand notes and type for him if he had, say, attended a conference in New York and wanted to have his report ready by the time he arrived in England.

This private service was usually rewarded with an extremely nice present at the end of the voyage.

Qualifications required for this exciting adventure were, mainly: (1) a minimum of two years' experience in an office; and (2) a foreign language, preferably French or Spanish, since part of the job was to collect together all the French (or Spanish) passengers and play hostess at a tea party to introduce them to each other. Whether they *wanted* to know each other or not didn't come into it.

The idea of a life on the ocean wave appealed to me, but not to my mother, however much I tried to pacify her with the thought that, after every round trip of 12 days, I would come back to Southampton and get home for a night or two, and after every four voyages I would get one voyage off, so she would see more of me than before …

As a child, I had been addicted to Captain Marryat's books, *Masterman Ready* and *Midshipman Easy*, and always read the sea stories in *Chums' Annual*, which I borrowed from a boy across the road, so joining the Merchant Navy would be a great thrill!

With high hopes, but not a little trepidation, I abandoned my lively journalistic colleagues and boarded a train to Liverpool for an interview with Cunard. Afterwards, my most impressive memories of the day were of passing a huge, blackened cathedral in the bus on the way to the Cunard Building, looking out on angry grey seas at the Pier-headland, waiting in an enormous room, full of busy people, where a short, stocky Liverpudlian suddenly materialised beside me, much to my embarrassment breaking into excruciating

French while expecting me to respond with all those people looking on.

It was no tea party. At the end of what he called 'our little chat', he said that a place in a ship would not be available for six months, and he'd like me to attend regular French conversation classes until I heard from him that he had a ship for me to go to.

Six months! Why had I been so precipitate in giving in my notice to the *Mail*?! I couldn't go crawling back ... Where was my next crust coming from? The only solution was to go to an agency and do 'temping' for the next six months. I might make a lot of new friends, and working in several different parts of London would broaden my knowledge of the great metropolis – like a taxi-driver.

In the 'Never-had-it-so-good' fifties, there were many flourishing employment agencies supplying temporary and permanent secretaries to firms all over London. Jobs galore abounded for anyone who could do shorthand and typing. Provided that you could pass the not-too-taxing test on your first visit to the agency, you were in. The agency charged the client about a quarter more than it paid the secretary, who, in turn, was usually paid more for temping than she got in a regular job, and everybody was happy (except, occasionally, some of the employers when they saw the bill).

The only trouble was that the agencies didn't really bother to fit the type of person to the type of job – well, they couldn't actually be expected to, since they had only been contacted on the telephone by an employer, and had met the secretary for 15 minutes at the most.

This, as will be disclosed, resulted in many square-peg-in-round-hole experiences, the only comfort being that one didn't have to stay in the job for long, and it was bearable if the end was in sight. However, if you really couldn't stand it, you could ask the agency to send you somewhere else after a week. The exciting part was that, if you were a single girl, still looking for 'Mr Right', you never knew whether you might find him in next week's job – and Hope sprang eternal in our (fairly) innocent breasts ...

> *'Today, I am alone in the squalid boredom of my eleventh temporary job. My only companion is a phantom machine in the corner, which coughs up cables from White Plains, New York. Every now and then it gives a sudden, angry buzz, and I rush at it and press knobs, but I always forget to push the one marked "Message Received" ... Can't you see the anxious faces at the other end, waiting in vain?'*

Thus I wrote to my friend Diana nearly three months later, as I, too, waited in vain for my ship to come in, and yearned for Fleet Street, lost for ever.

Shorthand Types was situated in the Strand and was run by a small, dark-haired woman, wearing a very short, pink skirt and a lot of false eyelashes, who interviewed me for five minutes and then handed me over to a heavily made-up minion who led me into another room and gave me a typing test which I managed to scrape through. (As I said, I didn't do much rapid typing in my job at the *Mail*.) Having told them that I would prefer to work for a publisher or Someone Literary, I was instructed to report to Screwbolt Engineering on the following Monday.

Screwbolt Engineering did not have a promising aspect: a creaking old wooden lift took me up to the third floor, where I was directed to a gloomy dark-green room, full of girls who all seemed to be trying out new hairstyles and painting their nails. Work was the last thing on their agenda. I was given nothing to do throughout that long, tedious day, and none of them had a word to say to me, except the one Irish girl, and you never find a speechless Irish girl …

In the afternoon a man came in briefly and said he'd "see me tomorrow". Tomorrow came, and we still did nothing for the first hour or so. Eventually, a little man came in and dictated, at top speed, a whole lot of technical jargon about pump cocks, which he instructed me to send to the Erection Department …

The Head Office was in Belfast and there were several other branches, so everything had to have carbon copies on yellow, green, pink, white and mauve paper. Since this was still in the days of typewriter rubbers and before photo-copiers, every time you made a mistake all these copies had to be rubbed out and corrected. It was the sort of office that was my worst nightmare: nothing worse could happen, so I thought, until the morning when I got stuck in the lift and spent what seemed like hours going up and down by myself until someone finally opened the doors and rescued me …

On Friday I decided that one week of nuts, bolts, pump-cocks, erections and the unfriendly, moronic girls had been enough, and, timidly, I asked Shorthand Types if I could work somewhere else. "Would you prefer ABC Television?" they asked. Now you're talking, I thought.

ABC Television had fabulous red-carpeted offices in Vogue House. There were a lot of bitchy girls in the lift, who chose not to answer when I asked them where to go. I was kept in Reception for an hour before I managed to persuade them that I was *not* a would-be television star waiting for an interview. At last, I was shown into a huge office with one girl who was ever so nice and neat – white shirt, navy blue skirt, perfect hair and flawless make-up – and a man who never spoke.

There was nothing to do all day … The girl, Tina, explained that they never had any work on Mondays. Tuesday was much the same. How could these firms afford to pay people to do nothing? No wonder Harold Macmillan kept telling us we'd never had it so good!

On Wednesday a script came in to be typed for *Admags Commercials*. This proved to be quite enlightening – when we got to it – but first came the dull grind of cutting stencils, typing and checking camera lists and make-up and wardrobe lists. The script, which was about gardening, turned out to be (unintentionally) Rather Rude, and the only gay spark in the place, a bouncy production assistant called Sally, came in and started acting it, with much giggling:

'Enter David with his Wolf Power Unit, playfully spraying Peggy.

Peggy: "Is it safe to do it, even when the grass is wet?"

David: "I've got lots of attachments ..."'

It continued in this vein, with more and more double-entendres as David suffered problems with his Wolf Power Unit until he finally learned how to use it and his lawn became soft and velvety.

We spent the rest of that day typing the script, and it was good to be occupied at last. Next day we packed crates, because they were moving out of central London to Teddington, so that job came to an end. They hadn't really needed me. Despite the red carpets, free tea, comfortable chairs and David with his Wolf Power Unit, it was really quite a relief to bid them farewell.

Easter intervened and, after a few pleasant days at home in rural Sussex, being cosseted by my over-anxious mother, Shorthand Types dispatched me to yet another place of work. This time, I found myself in the middle of an Atomic Spy Ring!

They said he was a publisher, but this man, who was definitely weird, turned out to be a second-hand bookseller, working in the tiniest house I had ever seen, in an alley off St Martin's Lane. It was reputed to have been Nell Gwynne's house, although the upstairs room was so small that one could not imagine how she managed to tumble about with Charles II, who, I believe was quite tall, and there didn't seem to be enough room for a bed. I had misgivings when I tapped on the low front door. A spruce, rosy-cheeked man opened it, and I could see immediately that he was rather odd. Facing me, right opposite the front door, was a lavatory and wash basin, all exposed to view: at least I wouldn't have to ask where it was, although I doubted whether I would use it if Mr Rosycheeks and I were to be working at such close quarters.

A small flight of stairs led upwards, a huge pile of books on each step, and the tiny upstairs room contained two desks, a bookcase, three chairs and a telephone. The whole place smelled rather nasty.

Mr Rosycheeks said that he had a Japanese friend who was using the office and would want to dictate, but was at present away. I discovered that the said friend was one of the four representatives of Japanese Atomic Energy at present visiting this country to make a £26-million deal for power stations with GEC (General Electric Co.).

How extraordinary that such important people should be using the smallest, scruffiest office in London! The friend must be the Japanese equivalent of Sir John Cockcroft ... so surely he should be entertained in much grander surroundings than Nell Gwynne's little love nest? My fertile imagination told me that this must be A Spy Ring! It was the middle of the Cold War, and we were all jumpy ...

The plot thickened: my new employer obviously wanted to have a secret conversation on the telephone, for we had hardly become acquainted when he sent me out to a coffee bar to have my elevenses – at 9.30. The coffee bar was run by a chatty old queer. When I returned, Mr Rosycheeks was sitting down with a vacuum cleaner in one hand and the telephone in the other, talking to someone called Maud. He hastily sent me out again to post a book on atomic energy addressed to someone in Moscow ... More and more suspicious. I made a note to tell my former colleagues in Fleet Street ...

As in all these temporary jobs, there seemed to be nothing to do. A young man with a fair moustache walked in and said that he was Mr R-C's pupil/assistant. He volunteered the information that he was penniless and had a pregnant wife. I warmed to him. The two of them went off somewhere together in the afternoon and left me alone. I sighed with relief, as it was so difficult to look busy and useful when there was nothing to do. Besides, I could spend a penny while they were out.

A man from the Army & Navy Stores came to mend the coffee percolator. These little domestic touches seemed more important to my employer than the bookselling (of which there wasn't much evidence). By this time, utterly convinced that 1 was in the middle of a spy ring, I telephoned Jack, my ex-colleague who was a Fleet Street science correspondent, always writing articles about atomic energy. Didn't he think it weird that these important officials, if they were who they said they were, were meeting in this squalid little hidey-hole and not at Claridges or somewhere similar? Jack told me to listen hard and report back to him each day. Then and there, we formed our own branch of MI5. This job was certainly streets ahead of Screwbolt Engineering and ABC Television in excitement value …

Unfortunately, we hadn't bargained for Mr Rosycheeks speaking fluent Japanese, so my would-be MI5 sleuthing operation was completely foiled by the fact that all conversations were held in Japanese and I learned nothing, but this atmosphere and the whole set-up continued to be odd and suspicious.

Shorthand Types must have either heard something or had some sixth sense, for they rang me up one day and asked if I was all right: I said I didn't think so, but couldn't explain. There was a silence, and then they said, "We'll have you out of there by the end of the week." What they had discovered, I never found out, but on my last morning, I arrived to find the whole place flooded. Yes, knee-deep in water.

Letters floated everywhere. I spent the morning trying to rescue these and dry them, while chatting to the Japanese visitors (in English, I hasten to add). The four of them sat on three chairs and drank sherry all the afternoon, which I had been instructed to give them. Mr Rosycheeks and his pupil did not put in an appearance: perhaps they were being interrogated by the real MI5 – or perhaps the Japanese atomic scientists had murdered them. That was the last I saw of Nell Gwynne's house, but I cannot hear her name mentioned, or even look at a basket of oranges without thinking of that one extraordinary week of my life.

Note: I recently heard Clive James make some crack about Japs liking to have tiny bedrooms – so perhaps this was all arranged to make them feel at home …?

Shorthand Types finally got it right and sent me to a publisher at last! Working for a publisher was considered very respectable and acceptable in High Society – that is, if you had to work at all, which was not remotely comprehended by some. A friend told me that when she yawned in the early hours of the morning at a Debs' dance, remarking that she really ought to go home as she had an early start in the morning, one of her companions shrieked in horrified tones, "You don't mean to say that you WORK!"

Anyway, where was I? Just entering the scruffy offices of Draft and Scribe, whose 'treasure', "Miss T. who's been with us 20 years", was off sick for a few weeks. Two delightful, elegantly-dressed gents, whom I will call Eton and Harrow, welcomed me warmly and, in a very short space of time, were initiating me into the mysteries of, alas, not publishing, but stocks and shares! They were absolutely obsessed with the Stock Market. The first half-hour of every morning was spent consulting the *Financial Times* and swapping secret tips which they had been given by friends in the City the evening before. I sometimes wondered if they ever went home, as so much financial advice was acquired the night before, but later gathered that these City chums were encountered on the homeward train journey.

They soon had me dabbling with my hard-earned pennies in small quantities of the shares which they recommended, one of which was Pillar Holdings, on which we all trebled our money. Under their guidance, I first sold half my shares, waited for them to rise again, and once more sold half, still keeping the original stake.

'Eton' was the Boss, who had his own office across the landing, to which I was politely summoned every now and then, when he wanted to dictate long letters to Head Office in Australia, or to authors and illustrators. His English was admirable, especially after the horrors of Screwbolt Engineering, and he dictated in a charming way, so that I savoured every word that I converted to shorthand and later reproduced as perfect prose on the ramshackle typewriter in the next room, which I shared with 'Harrow', who was extremely friendly, in a precious sort of way. His first act of kindness was to hand me two lumps of sugar for my tea, when it should arrive. I felt like a horse being given a treat (and hoped that I didn't look too much like one).

It was a pleasant surprise to find that tea was brought by a motherly minion in an overall, who carried it from somewhere downstairs to all the offices in the building, so for once I was not required to make it. Eton always stirred his tea with his spectacles, and usually came in for a chat (about shares, naturally) while drinking it. He loved his work, and the sounds of happy singing and occasional shouts of joy could be heard spasmodically from his room across the landing.

So much did I enjoy working there that I was very surprised to learn that the malady from which Miss T. was suffering was a nervous breakdown. I could not imagine that these two charmers could have driven her to it. When she returned, restored to health, they decided to keep me on, and split the job into two, as she was Getting On and they wanted to keep her going until she reached retirement age.

With her return, the levity and relaxed informality into which her two bosses had lapsed, which I had thought was their normal way of working, was NOT approved of, and we were all jerked into Better Behaviour. I did not find it easy to share what had been, until now, her life's work. Keeping the box of paper clips on one particular part of the mantelpiece, or using the carbon paper exactly six times before taking a new sheet were rituals which had become too vitally important to her …

They asked me to stay for ever, and I was tempted, but it *was* the coldest office in London, and that, combined with Miss T's frosty fetishes, the call of the sea for which I still waited, and the ever-burning hope of a husband waiting round the corner in the next job, or the one after that (Eton was married and Harrow *very* unlikely) caused me to leave after another six weeks.

The following Christmas I received a home-made Christmas card, drawn by Harrow, depicting my Austin 7 and a Rolls Royce side by side, bearing the caption, *'Before and after buying Pillar Holdings'*. I still have it.

At home one weekend, I went with my mother to a wedding, suffering the usual embarrassment of being older than the bride – and still with not even a boyfriend (or 'young man' as they were called in polite society) in sight. These weddings happened frequently in our village: one mother managed to get all her four daughters married 'to the right people' (a touch of *Pride & Prejudice* there) while I remained on the shelf.

Besides the question, asked pityingly, "Isn't your daughter thinking about marriage yet?" (She thought of nothing else, actually) the other question which irritated my mother beyond belief was, "What is your daughter *doing* now?" Or, to me, "What do you DO?" I longed to say that I was a Lady-in-Waiting to the Queen, or secretary to the Prime Minister (but we already had one of those in our midst), or engaged to a Duke, just to shut them up and get them to stop patronising my mother … 'Doing temporary work' didn't sound good at all.

Shorthand Types were beginning to recognise the sort of jobs that I would enjoy. They sent me to a magazine called *The Baker*, where I passed a hilarious week with a very amusing ex-Army officer turned Editor, who wrote a weekly column entitled *This Is Your Loaf*. (*This Is Your Life* was then in its heyday with Eamonn Andrews in his.) The Editor's secretary was, according to him, "away with a sore botty". For good measure, he added the information that she was a Jewess, and everything she ate had to be blessed by the Rabbi. Not even an unblessed biscuit could be consumed with her morning coffee ...

There were just three of us in the office: the Editor, the Advertisement Manager and me. The Advertisement Manager was a bit pernickety and wrote dozens of unnecessary letters, thanking people for thanking him for thanking them, just like a previous employer, and when they cancelled meetings, he wrote, somewhat florally, 'Meeting you is but a pleasure deferred ...' The Editor teased him unmercifully about a house which he had just bought "on an island", which turned out to be the Isle of Sheppey!

Other trade magazines inhabited the building and, when making coffee in the canteen, I made instant rapport with the secretary from *The Decorator*, with whom much laughter was enjoyed. Strange and sad how we meet kindred spirits for fleeting moments in our lives, for I never saw her again after that week, and do not remember her name, only that we delighted in sharing our humour.

I think I might have made progress with the Editor of *The Baker*, and even prised him away from his mother, with whom he lived in Hampstead, had I been there longer. Anyway, I did my best to stay in the same building, by trying to get a permanent job as Number 3 journalist on *The Outfitter*, but the Boss made me feel like Mrs Pankhurst chained to his desk when he said that he'd rather employ A MAN.

After this unedifying week, Shorthand Types sent me from the ridiculous to the sublime – a theatrical agency in the Strand, where everyone, including the men, called each other 'darling'. It ran true to form, being everything that one could imagine such an establishment to be. The boss, called Felix, sported a black moustache, bald head, white knitted tie, and gushed at everyone, even me.

I sat in the reception area and was doubled up with laughter at the antics of the switchboard girl, who answered the phone in a pseudo-plummy voice while making cockney comments out of the side of her mouth to us. She amused herself by cutting off the people she didn't like ("It's that old bitch again, I'll plug 'er up") and trying to corrupt the 15-year-old office girl in between calls. ("It's time you went on 'oliday with a man; in France and them countries they all do before they're 12 – it's good for you to 'ave Free Love.") She added that her boyfriend said he preferred blondes, "because they got dirty quicker"!

The great game was to pretend we didn't recognise the famous film stars when they came in, and to say, "What name, please?" which infuriated them.

One tedious afternoon I had to type a long, long letter (dictated by Felix) all about Anthony Steele's Income Tax. It seemed unbelievable that this gorgeous hunk of a man, whom I had only seen in a romantic light, from the red, plush seats of the one-and-nine-pennies, should have a problem with something so mundane as Income Tax.

Since the hoped-for call to a life on the ocean wave still did not come, I now had to be spirited away from the dramatic darlings to a Dirty Old Public Notary, called Mr N. Senior, and his supercilious son, called Mr N. Junior. There was horrible sweet tea and an executive key to the loo on the top floor, which caused endless comedy dramas, since no one must be seen approaching or leaving it if Mr N. Senior was around. In the office was a terrorised little girl messenger and quite a nice clerk.

I had to type complicated documents for Cypriots, who were all changing their names. One was a dossier on an old Cypriot woman who had been in prison for performing abortions. She stood there, grinning all over her ugly old face, while I typed it out.

Through the open windows, the mighty roar of London's traffic was added to by the buzz of helicopters, since the Paris Air Race of 1959 was going on.

There were wills in all languages, and no rubbing-out was allowed: at the first error, we had to start again. I wondered whether I would ever get *any*thing completed. The nasty old man was rude to all of us. According to the 17-year-old messenger-girl, he was missing his regular secretary (who was on 'oliday) because "she usually lets 'im '*ave* a bit". I hoped he wasn't expecting similar attention from me, as I worked away, typing death certificates in Polish and Portuguese while he quibbled over the size of envelope – but this was nothing to the fuss he made when he saw the size of my agency's bill!

He refused to speak to me for two days and then got round it by making me work an extra half-hour every day. When I left, the old hypocrite said he hoped I Had Been Happy there!

An entry in my diary for 25th of July, 1959, reads, '*Went to Gordon Boys' School to meet Monty'*. This was Field Marshal Montgomery, who was inspecting the Gordon Boys' School, near Woking, on their Speech Day, and since my mother was General Gordon's great-niece, I always got an invitation. It was hilarious how I ricocheted from being a humble typist, meekly suffering the slings and arrows of various employers, to spending Saturday with my relations, meeting some of the greatest in the land – and not daring to tell anyone in the office … We had tea in a marquee with Field Marshal Lord Alanbrooke, an old dancing partner of my mother's from the Indian days.

The following Monday, I took my small niece and nephew and put them on a plane to join their parents in a Middle-Eastern Embassy for the summer holidays and then repaired once more to see what horrible fate Shorthand Types had in store for the coming weeks.

Von Blowhorn Inc. was a London-based American company, designing and constructing engineering plants all over the world – in India, Japan, Yugoslavia, Argentina and Russia, to name but a few, for making nylon and rayon. Not my cup of tea at all, it was in a gloomy office in Kingsway, with very dim strip lighting. For the first three days I was instructed by the Austrian secretary, who had plenty of derogatory things to say about her American bosses. "Ze whole of the United States is one big bluff," she remarked.

Everything was very technical, with numbered files and cross-check files – you name it, it was there – and I had to go out and buy the stamps. In Fleet Street all letters had been franked by the postal department.

The old Yorkshireman who was supposed to be in charge instructed me not to get 'floostered', but the minute Miss Teller, the secretary, had departed on holiday, he became 'floostered' himself. He panicked and ran round in circles, looking in filing cabinets for things which didn't exist, and muddling me completely. Obviously, the firm's future was NOT safe in our hands for the next two weeks … He sent a cable saying, *'Request immediate return of Goodzeit; cannot carry on without him'*. Goodzeit, whoever he was, did not materialise.

Nothing happened for a few days. Then, one day, the phantom machine coughed up: *'Engage more staff and find new offices'*.

'Floostered' promptly rushed out and looked at several offices with impossibly high rents and, to fulfil the other half of the cable, turned to me and said, "You'll stay anoother moonth, won't you?"

The technical jargon was quite enlightening, if a little blush-making: on my first day, a young engineer put his head round the door and asked me if I had a catalogue of cocks. Then a letter came in, brightly headed, 'Flanged Plug Cocks', followed by a cable saying, *'Go easy on Erection Fees and Bed Rolls'*. Just as I was thinking that I never knew engineering could be so sexy, a young man telephoned and asked what my flow of acid water was. Really! There are limits! I was about to tell him not to be impertinent, when he explained that he was talking about a spin-bath – which might have been something used by the present government, only most of them weren't born then.

To keep the phantom machine going, I had to wrap a piece of paper round a cylinder and then this would revolve at speed until a cabled message appeared on it. The message might read: *'Your VST slash SN-UK-352 completely unsatisfactory. Airmail drawings and specifications for flange plug cocks immediately. Signed Head Office'*. Floostered would run round the room for half-an-hour, and then send back a cable saying, *'Cannot do what you ask'*. No reason given! That kept them quiet for a day, and then they started again. Had we received their message? (Once again, I had omitted to press the 'Received' button.)

They cabled, *'Refer to tolerance on Rolls and Erection Fee'*.

During the second week a typical stage American-German (or German-American) business tycoon called Winezieil arrived, en route between Head Office and Germany.

"Why haven't you guys done this, that, and the other? In the U.S. we get it the same day; here in England you take five weeks ..."

The old man got reet floostered and started shouting. They both shouted together for an hour without listening to each other, and then went out for coffee. This was after Winezieil had three times asked me to "go buy a pot of coffee", and we had explained three times that you can't (or couldn't then) do that here.

When they returned and I had dried my tears of laughter, Winezieil dictated masses of figures and technical jargon to my unwilling ears; so that there would be a record of his visit, because both he and I knew that the Old Man (I never knew his name) was not listening. I made a call to Germany for Winezieil and then he rang Mom and The Kids, told Mom to give the Kids more dough, said to her that he would find her somewhere, sometime, and flew off to Japan and out of my life. We had met for part of one day, and the experience had been as good as watching a Hollywood comedy.

Relief was sweet for me and for Floostered when Miss Feller (such a contradiction in terms) returned and I thankfully departed, leaving her to rectify all our mistakes. That was the joy of a temporary job, but otherwise it was an unstable and unsettled existence.

After a couple of dull jobs with accountants and actuaries in the City, I spent a fortnight in an attic on Laurence Pountney Hill, above Duck's Foot Lane, being passionately pursued by an extremely handsome German insurance broker. Every time I looked up from the typewriter, his lecherous eyes were on me ... He flattened me against the wall a few times, but somehow I got out of there unscathed, helped by the hunchbacked lift man, who was never far away from his task of pulling the ropes to make the lift go up and down.

Thinking that Cunard had forgotten me, I agreed to take a three-month job, helping to run the Boat Show at Earl's Court (or was it Olympia?). This was interesting, but there were no kindred spirits and I soon began to dislike my smarmy boss, so was absolutely delighted when at last the summons came, ordering me to join a slightly bigger boat than those in the Boat Show ...

WATER, WATER EVERYWHERE

AND FAR TOO MUCH TO DRINK

THE LETTER INSTRUCTED ME TO REPORT FOR duty in the *Queen Mary*, either at noon on Tuesday, or Wednesday of the following week – five days' notice! The reason for the choice of days was because they suggested that I ask their 'Social Directress' (for ever referred to by the Captain as their 'Social *Destructress*') for a lift down to Southampton as she lived near me, and it depended which day she chose to rejoin the ship. She was the most senior Lady Purser of all, and had been a Wren.

They enclosed a rail voucher in case I didn't get a lift, and many instructions about collecting my Discharge Book, my 'Seaman's' Identity Card and my uniform from Gieves, an expensive outfitter. This cost me £40 – a huge sum in those days. On my sleeves I proudly bore one gold ring, to show that I was an officer, and a white ring to denote the Purser's department. I was to register as a 'Seafarer' "when I had had my lunch"!

When I telephoned the number of the Social Directress, I found that she was the Rector's daughter from the next village. Small world indeed! Margaret Newcombe fetched me from my mother's cottage in her little old car on Tuesday, 12th April, 1960, and drove me all the way to the *Queen Mary*. She was a very comfortable person to be with and, by taking me with her, saved me from many anxious moments.

We went up the gangway and took a lift up to the First Class Purser's Office. She introduced me to everyone and then I was shown to my cabin on the Promenade Deck. I was to share with another new girl, from Birmingham. She was about twice my height, *very* self-assured, and wore spectacles with fly-away 'butterfly' tips, pointing upwards like a cow's horns, with little diamanté sparkly bits on them. I was thankful when she chose the top bunk: being at floor level meant that I could get out quickly if I felt sea-sick – or if the ship was sinking.

I was to work in First Class for the first few voyages. This was in the centre, or 'amidships'. My companion, another Margaret, was sent to Tourist

Class, which was right in the bows, where you felt the pitching, so I did not envy her. Nearly all the girls and most of the men came from Liverpool. There was a rule that men could start work when they were aged 18, but girls had to be over 24. I am not sure whether the management thought that this age difference would discourage romances between members of the Purser's staff, but it certainly didn't deter anybody …

Margaret Newcombe showed me round the whole ship. It rained all day, but I went ashore to sign on, and bumped into the man who had originally interviewed me. Back at the ship, he blew them all up for letting me go ashore alone. I had noticed that the eyes of the policeman at the dock gate had nearly dropped out when I said "Crew" as I passed him.

In the evening there was nothing to do, so some of us went ashore again to see Emlyn Williams playing excerpts from Dickens, and then went to a Coffee Bar.

Due to report in the office next morning at nine o'clock, I was horrified to discover that my watch was an hour slow, and I had 15 minutes to put on my uniform and get down there. No chance of breakfast, since it was 10 minutes' walk to the dining saloon. In the office they pounced on me and practically re-dressed me, tying my tie correctly and laughing at my over-sized shirt collar (we wore men's shirts). We sorted out the post and then had boat drill, which consisted of standing in a line on the inner deck while the Staff Captain inspected us. I never even saw a lifeboat; although I was told that sometimes they did the whole thing properly, letting the boats down into the water with us in them. I was thankful that this didn't happen, as we were so high up – apparently, the same height as Nelson's Column.

I was told that I was 'detailed' for leave after four trips, and that we always had to take every single possession home, because we changed cabins, or even ships, after every leave. We also changed jobs from one class to another, or to the Travel Bureau, which usually had two or three girls running it. Besides First and Tourist, there was Cabin Class, which was between the two and seemed to be chosen by the nicest passengers, of middle income. I was lucky enough to work in Cabin Class during most of my time at sea.

The Cabin Purser was also the Entertainments Purser some of the time. Dickie Davies was extremely good fun, and later had a career in television where he became well-known on *World of Sport*.

That first afternoon, we sorted out Chinese decorations (for some unremembered reason) while the Cabin Purser read nonsense rhymes to us in an assumed North Country voice until teatime, after which I was summoned to the Bridge to take dictation from the Staff Captain.

Next morning I got up in time, but got lost on the way to breakfast. The ship was so vast, and all the corridors looked the same. On duty with Sue

Macdonald, the charming Senior Lady Assistant Purser (another ex-Wren), I helped to welcome the passengers aboard at 10 a.m. Mostly returning Americans, all sorts of peculiar figures in outlandish clothes appeared. Among them were some sweet black babies and some typical old ladies with blue rinses, mostly asking the whereabouts of their cabins and depositing their valuables for me to put in the safe. One of these women confused me utterly by asking if there was a 'soda fountain' in her cabin, as her travel agent had assured her that there would be one. I hadn't the faintest idea what a soda fountain was, and desperately referred her to one of my male colleagues.

One man made a great scene and said that He Was Disgusted – but we never gathered what he was disgusted *about*!

We stayed on duty until 9.00 p.m., just dashing down for quick meals. All this time we were crossing the Channel. At Cherbourg there was a lot of fuss because the newspapers hadn't arrived and a passenger's third Cadillac had broken down in Paris. We only anchored outside, and didn't actually go into Cherbourg.

A jolly young Purser called Dudley, with a violent stammer and a very kind heart, walked about all day with a notice that someone had stuck on his back, saying, 'Not To Go'. He was completely oblivious of the titters that this was raising. Practical jokes never ceased, and neither did our laughter. We put the clocks back twice, and it was a very long afternoon. There seemed to be so many ships in the Channel that I asked Dudley about the possibility of a collision. "D-don't worry," he said, "it won't affect us, 'cos we're the b-b-biggest."

Horror struck the next morning as we woke feeling terrible, with the ship rocking violently. We had emerged from the English Channel into the Atlantic, and it was really rough! I just wanted to roll off the bunk and die! We took it in turns to be sick in the basin, and then collapsed once more into our bunks. It was past nine and we were still unable to lift our heads. Sue put her head round the door and asked, "Is anyone alive in here?" We were incapable of speech. A nurse, alerted by Sue, appeared with some blue pills. Later, a very kind Steward (not John Prescott) arrived with a plate of dry biscuits and sandwiches. "It'll do yer good to eat something, luvs." I wished I had never come …

By the afternoon I had recovered enough to go on the Sun Deck, and was surprised to see that the dreaded Atlantic was now quite calm. I even did two hours in the office. A mad American woman telephoned from her cabin and would not give her name, but I managed to straighten out her problem. Once over my initial nerves, I regarded the passengers' queries as an enjoyable challenge. We all competed to see how many people's names we knew by the end of the four-and-a-half-day voyage.

Late that night I went for a walk on the Sun Deck (by moonlight) with two of the other girls and we visited the dog passengers in their row of large cages. They looked beautiful, but sad, as only dogs can look, especially a large bulldog.

The following day, my health fully restored, I got up early and went on deck before breakfast. One of the men put us all off by having onion soup for breakfast (you could choose absolutely anything you liked) and I soon learned that onion soup was a well-tried cure for a hangover! It was quite rough, but the ship's manifests had to be typed. We sat on high stools with our typewriters on the counter. Every now and then, when the ship rolled violently, the typewriter would slide down the counter and one would have to grab it back. The *Queen Mary* took several minutes to roll from one side to the other and back.

Our typing was constantly interrupted by passengers' queries, and we had to make sure that they filled in their immigration forms correctly before arrival in New York. These caused quite a lot of amusement: one man, in answer to 'Sex?' wrote 'white', while another wrote 'sometimes' … A New Zealand sheep farmer, travelling First Class and said to be one of the richest men in the world, signed his name with an X. Many of them seemed to have no knowledge of geography, and one woman, when asked if she had boarded the ship at Southampton or Cherbourg, answered vaguely, "Oh, well, I guess it was the second stop," as if we were a bus. Another *insisted* that she had boarded the ship in *Paris*! In vain did we tell her that there was no sea in Paris, and the *Queen Mary* would not fit in the Seine.

Very conscious of my senior officers listening in, I dealt with my first French passenger without any misunderstandings, and then the ship's doctor introduced himself and the world shrank once more as I learned that one of our old doctors at home was his father-in-law!

On the 17th of April I sent a greetings cable to my mother for her birthday, actually watching it go off from the Wireless Room.

That evening we went to a Midland Bank cocktail party. The Midland had a branch in each of the three classes. They ran the party in style, having a frock-coated young man calling out our names as we entered their very grand cabin. At the *Daily Mail* I had known a journalist called Rhona Churchill, whose husband was a Midland Bank manager. They surprised me by saying that they knew him, and that he had started his career on a ship, like them.

We stood throughout the party, and the rough sea made it quite hard not to overbalance. We ended the evening in very comfortable seats at the cinema, as we did most nights, for they changed the films frequently.

On Sunday we attended the Church service in the Main Lounge. Every Sunday we had the same hymn, 'Eternal Father, strong to save, whose arm hath bound the restless wave, etc., for those in peril on the sea', and now, whenever I hear it, I am reminded of those Sundays in the *Queen Mary*'s Main Lounge.

It was a hectic afternoon, as I was trying to type a speech for a passenger, and was constantly interrupted by people with queries, and, to top it all, the Staff Captain suddenly asked me to go up and read French to him. There were only two of us on duty.

Most of the time, the girls were not allowed to mix with the passengers during the evening entertainments, but the boys had to be sociable and dance with them. There was a very strict rule that you must *never* be rude to a passenger, and it was thought that there might be a situation where a man got fresh with a Lady Purser and she had to insult him (or even slap his face) in self-defence, and this was best avoided altogether by not letting us be present at all.

However, there was *one* night when passengers were invited to make themselves an original hat which represented the title of a well-known song, and two Lady Assistant Pursers had to be present to assemble the passengers into a line, write down their names and note the winners. All through the day, the would-be contestants queued up at our counter with requests for coloured crêpe paper and other materials. I enjoyed myself, drawing pictures on the blackboard of suggested examples, but one of my male colleagues was a brilliant artist, who came up with some real winners. The passengers produced some ingenious creations: one man wore a pair of black tights on his head as *Black Bottom* (a popular dance tune in America), another wore a wig and earrings as *I Enjoy Being A Girl*. One of my suggestions was a bird's nest with an egg in it, to represent *Younger than Spring Time*.

A warm, sunny day followed, most of which I missed, because I had to take dictation from a German Professor, which kept me busy inside until 8.20 p.m., but he was charming, and gave me my first 'tip' of a dollar!

Suddenly, we were almost there! The great US of A! Early in the morning we could see a skyline which, I was told, was Rockaway Beach. We quickly approached New York ...

The scene was chaotic, as everyone was getting ready to disembark and piles of luggage mounted up, close to where the gangways would be. We were so frantically busy that I hardly got a chance to see anything outside the ship, but I dashed into Margaret Newcombe's cabin to see the Statue of Liberty – a rather overrated green lady, waving her arm in the air – and into the Doctor's cabin to have a hasty glimpse of the Empire State Building and Rockefeller Center.

Amid a noise from the hooters like an orchestra's overture, we docked at Pier 90, and there were all the cars, dashing along, interspersed with hundreds of bright yellow taxis. As a newcomer, I had to have my fingerprints taken by the Immigration Authorities.

The Purser kindly let me off duty at 3.00 p.m., so that I could dash up the road with the other girls past seamy, blackened tenements with scruffy children sitting outside on the steps, uphill out of the dock area, hopping on a bus to the smart shopping area. Bus fares were all the same, no matter how far you were going, which struck me as a good idea. We went to a shop called Alexander's, where we bought our white summer uniform. No one would believe it now, but I took size eight. We trailed to Macy's (a glorified Selfridges) and Lane's (more like C & A).

After this, we sat on stools in Woolworth's and drank the most delicious hot chocolate that I have ever had. It was grander than our Woolworth's, and we even had supper there, before going to see *Can-Can* on Broadway.

I felt sure that arriving by sea and exploring the much-hyped City of New York on foot was far more interesting than flying in. Everywhere huge banners proclaimed that New York was the 'Greatest City in the World' etc., etc., but I must confess that, in daylight, my first impression was one of disappointment. I had expected clean and sparkling skyscrapers, but it was really rather grubby, the streets were narrow, Broadway was not broad, and buildings which were not skyscrapers were very low. Their shop windows were not carefully arranged like ours; everything just seemed to have been thrown in together in a muddle. Fifth Avenue was the exception; here, expensive and glamorous garments were tastefully displayed.

However, when the lights came on in Broadway, it seemed like a mad film, and the picture was completed by the sight of a police car simply *screaming* down Fifth Avenue.

On the return journey they let me loose on the counter unsupervised, and I feared that some passengers might end up in prison as a result of my having attended to their immigration papers. However, confidence was slowly growing and I was really enjoying the experience.

Our ship's orchestras were run by the famous 'Geraldo', and he introduced black bow ties for the Lady Pursers (usually known as Lady A/Ps) to wear in the evenings.

My cabin mate was driving me mad, and the others were all in sympathy with me when I told them of our nightly battles: she was dead against fresh air, and stuffed a pillow into the porthole each night. In the early hours I would wake with a splitting head, and crawl across our tiny cabin to remove the pillow, whereupon she would shout and yell and climb down the ladder (wearing a nightcap and spectacles) to replace the pillow … The knowledge that I should have to endure three more voyages of this before we could be separated was hard to bear!

However, there were more important things to deal with as we prepared for the return journey to Southampton. Pandemonium set in as each passenger brought about 20 friends aboard to see them off. Little girls resembling pet poodles were dressed in long, frilly pantaloons under frilly dresses and non-passengers were swarming all over the ship. We had quite a job making sure that all those visitors got off the ship again before we sailed. Apparently, there was nearly always a stowaway, and it was part of the social chit-chat to ask, "Have you met the stowaway this trip?"

I was told that some members of the crew never went ashore at either end, because they were wanted by the police or the Inland Revenue and could have been apprehended if they set foot on dry land.

In no time we were on the open sea again and I was taking dictation from a man who was writing very funny character-sketches of Paris butchers in Les Halles. He gave me a present of a sausage – not now among my souvenirs …

Once more, I was dealing with hundreds of manifests: one man had put down his country of birth as 'Hungry' and his occupation as 'mainly eating and sleeping'. I felt a bit seasick and was advised to drink Canada Dry ginger ale, which really did work and was a useful bit of advice for the future. After lunch on the third day, the doctor lurched up to the counter, very much the worse for wear, and kept repeating, "You come from Shushex – listen everyone, she comes from Shushex," while the Purser tried to pull him away. Sometimes the doctor came in to breakfast announcing that he would "just have the pudding". He really didn't know the time of day!

On this voyage we had a family of Knickerbockers and a passenger whose Christian name was Cactus. I had to learn not to say "Christian name", but *first* name, for fear of offending Jews and other religions.

One of the little 'bell-hops' or messenger-boys made a very profound remark about religion in this context: he said, "We all use different brands of soap powder, but we're all believing in the same thing; cleanliness."

I did four hours' typing for a British Motor Corporation salesman who had known the *Daily Mail* motoring correspondent. He gave me a box of chocolates and said he was not surprised that I had run away to sea …

Approaching Cherbourg, I was up early enough (5.30 a.m.) to see the pilot leaping from a small boat and climbing up a ladder which hung from the ship's side. We stayed in Cherbourg all day, busily writing out landing cards for passengers who were allowed ashore until 4.00 p.m. We had broken the average daily speed record since 1938! – 30.02 knots (the *Daily Express* got it wrong and said 32 knots). This meant that we had to hang about the Channel, crawling across, because we weren't due in Southampton until midnight. I made friends with the French Customs officer, who gave me some little sample bottles of scent. After that, he brought me some every time.

I was pursued round the deck by a bearded Sikh – the pursers roared with laughter as I tore into the office for refuge. We were on duty for 18 hours that day, with very little time to eat anything. Colleagues grabbed sandwiches and brought them to us. My uncle picked me up next morning and took me out to his house in Ringwood, where I had a luxurious night in a proper bed – with the window open! Then it was a bus ride back to the ship, and we sailed again at lunchtime. After making several crossings of the Atlantic, we tended almost to forget which way we were going.

We passed a busy morning in the Post Room, sorting out all the letters for the passengers and putting them into alphabetical pigeonholes. There were several interesting passengers: Ambassadors and other diplomats, a delegation from Ghana, all wearing brightly-coloured robes; a woman MP, Lady Tweedsmuir, was also travelling (not in bright robes) and poor Lord Audley, who dictated letters to me from his bed, as he had just suffered a stroke and couldn't write. He signed his letters with a funny drawing of himself. Sarah Churchill, Winston's actress daughter and Lord A's friend, was looking after him. They were both charming to me.

The majority of the passengers embarked at Cherbourg in the afternoon, and I rescued a lost Frenchman who couldn't find his cabin. We had received an order from on high to dump 3,000 packs of cigarettes at sea because they were packed in old-fashioned cartons and not the new design. What a terrible waste, we thought, and half the crew was itching to get their hands on them.

On the 1st of May we went into 'whites', although it was rather a horrible day. An American couple asked me to type a long list of everything that they had bought on their travels round Europe, so that they could show it to the Customs people. They gave me a three-dollar tip.

Life became more and more pleasant in the calm summer months. Sometimes we saw the *Queen Elizabeth*, going the other way. We were not allowed to pass within 12 miles of each other. We also saw the *United States*, but seldom any other ships until we got near land.

There were always interesting passengers, from Leopold Stokowski to Donald Swann (of Flanders and Swann fame), who was very nice; Lady Docker, about whom some unrepeatable stories were told; Hermione Gingold, who sat on her cases while she waited to land at New York, singing "I'm glad I'm not young any more"; T. S. Eliot, A. L. Rowse, Hardy Amies and many more famous names of that era.

On different voyages we all swapped occupations in various departments. I even played a double bass, constructed from a tea chest and some bits of string, in the children's orchestra which we organised to make their tea party more exciting. Once, in Tourist Class, we had a criminal who was being deported back to the United States, guarded by three British policemen. It was all supposed to be a Big Secret, but a *Daily Express* man came aboard at Southampton and started asking questions. With a perfectly straight face and the Purser treading heavily on my foot under the counter, I said, "Oh, no, we've nobody of *that* name on board."

By now, on subsequent visits to New York, I had done all the usual touristy things, such as going up to the top of the Empire State Building and looking at the *Queen Mary* through a telescope from there, eating the most delicious food in a Japanese restaurant, buying miniature radios the size of a cigarette packet for very little money, and visiting the wonderful St Patrick's Cathedral.

Once, we visited an Irish restaurant where all the tablecloths were emerald green and we drank peppermint to match. Having a drink in the Rainbow Room on the 66th floor of Rockefeller Center was also something to talk about.

Late that summer there was a seamen's strike, and all the catering staff joined in, so we had to get our own food. I also remember being stuck in the Channel because it was too windy for the tender to bring the passengers out to us off Cherbourg. There was nothing to do, so we made Christmas decorations; as I wrote to my mother, '*I have just made a Reindeer …*' To relieve our boredom, the Staff Purser sat in his little window, looking out from his office, wearing a woman's hat covered in large paper roses, saying in an American accent, "My Travel Agent told me to sit right here until he came to fetch me."

And then, that autumn, there was The Hurricane – called 'Donna'. Ropes were put up all over the ship for people to hang on to, but even so, 13 passengers broke ribs and a few broke other things. I know this, because I had to type all the Accident Reports and stagger repeatedly down to the hospital in the bowels of the great ship, to get them signed by the doctors.

I was one of the few people who were still on their feet, and I had to give my French tea party! It was hilarious, as only one man came, from the French Sudan, and as we tried desperately to carry on some small talk in French, he slowly turned from black to green and departed in a hurry, just as I had poured out the tea …

But that, to my great relief, was the end of the party.

Instead of going *round* the hurricane, our gallant Captain had decided to charge right through the middle of it, at speed … It was certainly an exciting experience. One passenger, sitting in a chair, went over backwards, chair and all.

If other Cunard ships were docked in New York, we went to parties in them, and met old colleagues who had been transferred. One of our Purser's

Clerks woke up on a sofa aboard the *Britannic* at 9.15 the next morning, wearing a life jacket – it had certainly been a good party! The *Britannic* was broken up after that (not because of the party).

One evening in Southampton, as I stood behind my counter, besieged by about 400 passengers, all asking questions at once, a breathless Baggage Master erupted into their midst, gasping, "Have you seen two Great Danes pass this way?" We hadn't, but the situation was desperate, for they had jumped out of the van which was delivering them to the ship. When the van-driver opened the doors, they leapt over his head and disappeared along the docks. One was the Champion of Crufts and the other was his 'wife'. She was soon recaptured, but her 'husband' did not reappear until just before we sailed next morning, having had a night out in Southampton.

There was one cruise ship, the *Caronia*, which went right round the world, but only two Lady A/Ps worked on it, so it took approximately four years for one's turn to come, and many of us left before that, either to get married or because dashing to and fro across the Atlantic bashing a typewriter began to pall.

Moonlight is usually associated with romance, but in my case it was the wrong kind of moonlight: somehow, we never managed to save much money while we were at sea, even though we had no living expenses. It all seemed to go in New York, so during our frequent leaves, some of us, probably illicitly, did temporary jobs to earn a little extra on the side. Therefore, I happened to be 'moonlighting' in a sumptuous carpeted office in a glass-fronted building on the site of the old Stoll Theatre where, long ago, I had stood up with my friend Diana and yelled and clapped and shouted "Bravo!" with everyone else at the end of a brilliant performance of Verdi's *La Forza del Destino*, when I came face to face with my future husband!

Had I known what was happening to me at that moment, I might well have repeated the frenzied cheering of that unforgettable evening in my youth …

He had just arrived at the office, and was wearing a bowler hat above his City suit. His face was just the right shape for it, and he looked devastating. Immediately we had been introduced and he had been told that I was there to work for his colleague temporarily, while on leave from the *Queen Mary*, he launched into one of his funny stories, of which he had a vast repertoire (I would be listening to them for the next 30-odd years). I may not have remembered all the details correctly, but in essence it was the one about the American and the Englishman, vying with each other in boasting about their respective countries' ships.

"Our liners make yours look like little pleasure boats," swanked the yank. They were standing on the docks at Southampton. The Englishman caught sight of the *Queen Mary* advancing up the Solent. He thought for a minute, then, cupping his hands like a loud hailer, he bellowed, "Come in Number 23, your time is up!"